Readings in
Income Taxation

LS 360715

- PAUL BORG -
  D - 617-338-3621
  H - 617-247-3886
  - KEYSTONE INUST CARD -

TAMMY - Charleston
803-851-9729 ofVer 9:10
- GAP INS -

AY

(5) A6 -

3369
5841
1338
2450
2515
15513.

134 3/4
99
SFPM 133/8
62 7/8

160 4 6
MOT 50 7/8

Huebner School Series — *Gary K. Stone, Editor*

The primary purpose of this series is to provide timely reading materials tailored to the educational needs of those professionals pursuing the Chartered Life Underwriter and Chartered Financial Consultant designation programs offered by the Solomon S. Huebner School of The American College. These publications should also be of interest to other persons seeking further knowledge in the broad area of financial services.

Huebner School Series

Readings in
Income Taxation
Thirteenth Edition

Edited by James F. Ivers III

The American College/*Bryn Mawr, Pennsylvania*

This publication is designed to provide accurate and authoritative information about the subject covered. The American College is not engaged in rendering legal, accounting, or other professional service. If legal or other expert advice is required, the services of an appropriate professional should be sought.

Library of Congress Catalog Card Number 89-640071
ISBN 0-943590-77-9

Printed in the United States of America

Contents

Acknowledgments

I wish to express my gratitude for the editing by Emily C. Sims; the dedicated support of Patricia G. Berenson for her capable assistance and for typing the manuscript; and the excellent graphics of Howard E. Hoctor, all of The American College.

A word of thanks is also extended to Fred J. Dopheide, former vice president of Educational Resources at the American Society of CLU & ChFC, for his assistance and helpful comments.

In addition, I would like to acknowledge the support and encouragement of Gary K. Stone, PhD, CLU and C. Bruce Worsham, JD, LLM, CLU.

To these individuals and to the many capable instructors, students, and friends whose constructive suggestions have been incorporated in this book of readings, I express my appreciation and gratitude.

James F. Ivers III

Readings in
Income Taxation

Access to Sources of Tax Law and New Legislation

James F. Ivers III

INTRODUCTION

A student or financial services professional will frequently need information regarding a particular issue or new piece of legislation in the area of federal income taxation. This reading will ease the process of basic tax research and point out means of access to new law and related explanatory material.

Effective research of court decisions involves techniques that are beyond the scope of this reading. However, the use of the basic tax services, encyclopedias, periodicals, and material published on new law is appropriate for the student.

The basic services and encyclopedias are well worth their substantial cost, which includes annual charges for periodic revisions. However, unless the student is a specialist in taxation, he or she is likely to use these services at a library.

MAJOR TAX SERVICES

Three of the major reporting services in the area of federal income tax are

- *Federal Tax Coordinator 2d,* published by The Research Institute of America (RIA)
- *Federal Taxes 2nd,* published by Prentice-Hall
- *Standard Federal Tax Reporter,* published by Commerce Clearing House (CCH)

Each of these services consists of multivolume sets with updates provided regularly in the form of replacement sheets or add-ons for the loose-leaf format each service uses.

Each includes the Internal Revenue Code sections and the current regulations promulgated thereunder. In addition, each includes explanatory material and case citations or annotations that summarize court decisions and provide references to the full text of opinions related to a particular subject or issue.

The RIA service is organized by topic, and volumes run alphabetically in sequence. To find the volume letter for a particular topic, the researcher must consult the index volume.

The Prentice-Hall and CCH services are organized by sequential treatment of Internal Revenue Code sections. Both Prentice-Hall and CCH contain a thorough subject index volume.

It may be easier for the fledgling researcher to use the RIA service, since it is organized by subject and contains lengthy explanatory text. The RIA service offers a *Practice Aids* volume, which contains tax ideas along with reprints of IRS audit manuals. It also provides two volumes of proposed regulations as well as reprints of recent revenue rulings and revenue procedures.

The Prentice-Hall and CCH services, on the other hand, offer more verbatim reprints of various elements of primary-source tax law. Both offer more extensive annotations of court decisions. CCH also offers a two-volume *Citator* that shows where each listed decision has been cited and discussed in later court decisions.

Each service has its own advantages and character. The researcher will likely become more familiar with one and will develop a preference based on that familiarity. All three services (and others) can be found in most law libraries, as well as in other selected libraries.

The researcher should note that all three services are referenced by paragraph number, not page number. The upper corner of each page contains the paragraph numbers, while the page numbers appear in the bottom corner of the page.

ENCYCLOPEDIAS

Two of the major encyclopedia-type multivolume tax treatises are Rabkin and Johnson, *Federal Income, Gift, and Estate Taxation,* and Mertens, *Law of Federal Income Taxation.*

Rabkin and Johnson is a 12-volume treatise organized by subject and is characterized by its economy of language and its clear explanatory material. It is supplemented monthly. Rabkin and Johnson includes congressional committee reports to inform the researcher of legislative history with respect to various Code sections. It is also available in a single-volume desk edition, which is a condensed version of the full encyclopedia.

Mertens is a 15-volume reference source characterized by its thoroughness in the treatment of each Code section and its highly detailed explanatory text. It is also organized by subject. Mertens is supplemented monthly to reflect new developments. It also provides additional volumes containing the Internal Revenue Code, all Treasury regulations, and all revenue rulings promulgated under the Internal Revenue Code of 1986 and subsequent amendments. Mertens also offers two additional volumes entitled *Code Commentary,* which feature explanations of each section of the Code in simplified language.

Both encyclopedias are of high quality. Preference is generally based on familiarity.

PERIODICALS

There are a host of periodicals that publish tax articles, and this reading is not intended to recommend a selective list over any others.

Commerce Clearing House publishes *Federal Tax Articles,* a comprehensive list of tax-related articles published in all types of professional journals.

Among the periodicals devoted exclusively to taxation are the *Journal of Taxation, Taxes — The Tax Magazine, Tax Notes,* and the *Monthly Digest of Tax Articles.*

The *Journal of the American Society of CLU & ChFC* also publishes many tax-related articles in addition to other articles of interest. Numerous other periodicals include tax articles of interest to the financial services professional.

NEW LEGISLATION AND RELATED MATERIAL

Each of the three major tax services publishes verbatim reprints of new tax legislation and accompanying legislative history, explanatory material, and analysis. These separate volumes can be obtained by contacting the publishers.

Within the basic tax services are sections covering current developments. Volume 12 of Prentice-Hall is entitled *Recent Developments* and contains new legislation, recent cases, and rulings that have not yet been incorporated into the main body of the service. Prentice-Hall also includes committee reports on new legislation and its weekly report bulletins in this volume. Volume 16 of CCH, entitled *New Matters,* contains materials similar to those in volume 12 of Prentice-Hall. It also includes a cumulative index to new developments. Additional volumes of CCH provide advance sheets on court decisions in tax cases in the federal courts.

The RIA service contains a tab section at the end of each volume entitled "Developments." This section features decisions, rulings, and other developments occurring since the last periodic revision. The new developments are referenced by way of specific paragraph numbers to the main body of the service.

In addition to materials published by the major tax services, major accounting firms also publish summaries of each new piece of federal tax legislation. These are generally easy to read, although depth of coverage is not comparable to the publications of the major services. However, these summaries can be quite satisfactory for an overview of the highlights of new tax legislation. They are generally available by contacting the local office of major accounting firms shortly after new tax legislation is signed by the president.

The definitive printed report for the latest tax developments is the *Daily Tax Report,* published by the Bureau of National Affairs (BNA). The *Daily* is thorough, well written, and appropriate not only for the tax specialist but also for the financial planner.

CCH has a data base service that provides quick access to the latest developments in all areas of tax law. This service is called "CCH ACCESS." For information regarding features, cost, and computer compatibility, contact the publisher.

There is also a tax data base service called TAXRIA that is available as a part of the LEXIS service, a legal research data base.

CONCLUSION

A few trips to the tax section of a law library will make the student familiar with the ways in which tax law is developed and reported. In view of the importance of tax matters in virtually every aspect of the financial planning process, basic research techniques should be of interest to the student.

2

A History of the Income Tax Law and a Glance at the Sources of Current Law

Stephan R. Leimberg[*]

EARLY TAX LAW

The tax history of the United States mirrors the general history of this country. Under the Articles of Confederation, the first governing instrument adopted by the Continental Congress in 1777, the federal government had no taxing power or right to collect custom duties. Several attempts to amend the Articles and give Congress a power to tax failed.

Because the Articles of Confederation proved to be too weak, the Constitution, written in 1787 and ratified in 1789, enlarged the powers of the federal government. However, the framers of the Constitution feared that the accumulation of power by the federal government would result in tyranny similar to the absolute monarchy of King George III of England. Therefore the government was divided into three coequal branches of government (legislative, executive, and judicial) with a system of checks and balances. The original taxing power of the federal government under the Constitution was sharply limited by the uniformity and apportionment clauses—Article I, Sections 8 and 9 of the Constitution. A detailed explanation is beyond the scope of this reading, but it is sufficient to say that these clauses, in retrospect, precluded the federal government from imposing an income tax.

INCREASED PRESSURE FOR REVENUES

The high cost of the Civil War brought about the first governmental attempt to collect a tax on income. The tax soon expired, but by 1894 governmental needs for revenue led to the adoption of another income tax. Within a year, the constitutional validity of this tax was tested. In the famous case of *Pollock v. Farmers' Loan and Trust Company,* the U.S. Supreme Court held that the tax was

---

*Stephan R. Leimberg, JD, CLU, is professor of taxation and estate planning at The American College.

neither apportioned among the states nor uniform and was therefore unconstitutional, as Pollock had claimed.

Congressional reaction to the *Pollock* decision was shaped by the increasing pressures as well as the demands for a steady and sufficient source of revenue. The result was a political compromise in 1909 that levied a tax on corporations. However, even while the constitutionality of the Revenue Act of 1909 was being considered, Congress realized the need for a broader tax base.

THE 16TH AMENDMENT

In 1909, the 16th Amendment to the Constitution, which nullified the *Pollock* decision, was adopted by Congress. After appropriate action by the states, it was declared ratified on February 25, 1913. The 16th Amendment says the following:

> The Congress shall have the power to lay and collect taxes on income, from whatever source derived, without apportionment among the several States, and without regard to any census or enumeration.

It is this amendment that dispensed with the apportionment requirement and therefore became the foundation for the basic framework of our modern tax law. The broad and sweeping language that permitted "income, from whatever source derived" to be taxed pervades the entire income tax law and has far-reaching implications.

Congress quickly utilized the newly sanctioned revenue source. The corporate income tax created by the Revenue Act of 1909 was discontinued. Individuals, as well as corporations, then became subject to the broad new income tax introduced by Congress in 1913.

THE CODE

The Revenue Act of 1913 was quickly followed by a series of additional revenue acts. In 1939 the entire federal tax law was codified and entitled the Internal Revenue Code of 1939. The crucial need to raise revenue to finance World War II turned the income tax from a tax on wealthy taxpayers to a tax on the majority of the population. This period also saw the introduction of the withholding provisions for employees. After the war the Code provisions were rearranged and revised. The result was the Internal Revenue Code of 1954. The Code is now called the Internal Revenue Code of 1986, however, as a result of the voluminous changes wrought by the Tax Reform Act of 1986. Numerous additional changes have been made since 1986.

FUNCTIONS OF THE INCOME TAX SYSTEM

Revenue-Producing Function

The income tax law originated as a revenue-producing mechanism to supply money for the administration and operation of the federal government. The bulk of the government's net receipts are still produced by the federal income tax. Congress, however, does not enact tax laws solely to raise revenue. The tax law also serves economic, social, and regulatory functions.

Economic Function

The Internal Revenue Code plays an important role in the management of the nation's economy. According to current economic thinking, greater taxes result in lower spending by consumers. The reasoning concludes that by reducing consumer spending (without increasing governmental expenditures) the income tax system can be used to reduce inflationary trends. Conversely, the use of tax incentives or lower tax rates leaves consumers with more cash that, in turn, translates into increased spending, saving, and investment. The hoped-for result is an increase in the national product that will increase the demand for new workers and thus reduce unemployment. Thus the tax system can prevent or reduce the impact of recessions.

Some economic experts feel that the very nature of a progressive income tax will automatically perform both anti-inflationary and antirecessionary functions without Congress actually changing the rates. The theory is that when more dollars (through increased salaries) are available to consumers, their income taxes will increase more than proportionately, resulting in a dampening of their ability to make inflationary expenditures with their increased incomes. During recession the amount of money collected through the federal income tax decreases more than proportionately as the amount of a taxpayer's income decreases. Thus the relative reduction in income available to taxpayers is less than the reduction in their wages and salaries. Consequently, recessionary forces should be smaller than they otherwise would be. However, at the present time, recessionary signs are not coupled with a reduction in salaries. The value of the dollar is continually being eroded. Salary increases push the taxpayer into increasingly higher tax brackets, leaving less spendable income than before. As a result, our progressive tax structure does not automatically provide an anti-inflationary function during the type of combined recession-inflation that the United States encountered in the 1980s.

Further, the Code used incentives to encourage economic activity at the taxpayer level. For example, liberal depreciation rules as well as an investment credit encouraged taxpayers to invest capital in their businesses that, in turn, created more jobs for the nation. These incentives are now being questioned.

Social Function

As the tax base grew wider and rates became higher, Congress found that in addition to producing revenue, the tax structure could be used as a method of effectuating governmental policy. For example, the income tax, as a progressive tax, could be used to redistribute the national wealth. A progressive tax is one in which the amount of tax increases more than proportionately as the amount of the taxpayer's taxable income increases. Therefore in theory, if not in practice, by taking a higher proportion of tax dollars from higher incomes rather than from lower incomes (and using those dollars for governmental expenditures that benefit lower income taxpayers), the distribution of national wealth could be changed significantly. The social function of the income tax has been increasing in importance.

Regulatory Function

The income tax system performs a regulatory function as well as the revenue and social functions mentioned above. Two extreme examples of this use of the tax system to discourage socially undesirable activities are the punitive tax on marijuana and the tax on automatic weapons.

Counterbalancing Factors

There are, of course, factors that shape the methods used to achieve these ends. Balancing the need of the federal government for revenues is the desire of Congress to be fair to the parties affected. Generally, *fairness* is recognized as being "equal treatment of equals" and reasonable differences in the treatment of unequals. The test of this fairness is how well the tax imposed matches a taxpayer's ability to pay. Counterbalancing a desire to be fair, Congress is keenly aware of the political consequences of its actions. For example, it is generally politically more expedient to tax a small and unorganized group of voters than to tax a large, organized group with an effective and well-financed lobby.

Thus a tax law is a compromise between purposes and people—with great pressures exerted by the economic, political, and social groups who are affected by particular laws, and who constantly lobby in Congress in an attempt to have tax laws changed to their advantage.

SOURCES OF TAX LAW TODAY

Each of the three coequal branches of the federal government has a major role in the federal income tax system. These roles can be shown graphically by the illustration below.

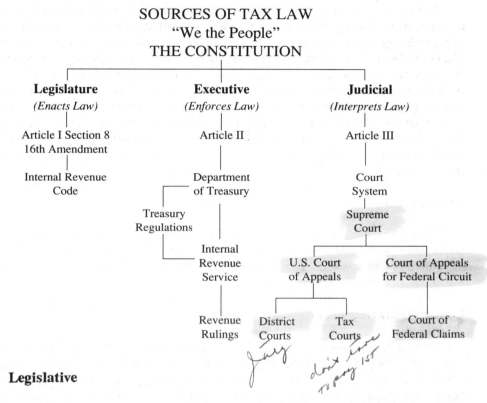

SOURCES OF TAX LAW
"We the People"
THE CONSTITUTION

Legislative

The 16th Amendment to the U.S. Constitution empowered Congress to enact an income tax law now compiled in the Internal Revenue Code. The importance of the Code is that federal taxation must proceed from a statutory origin. The present Code came into effect in 1986. It is revised and updated almost annually by Congress. Specific Code sections or parts of sections can be amended or repealed through the passage of revenue bills, which then supersede the older law as to those provisions. The House of Representatives has the constitutional responsibility for initiating revenue bills. A revenue bill becomes law, in most cases, through the following process:

- Revenue bills are written by the Ways and Means Committee of the House of Representatives, or bills are received by the Ways and Means

Committee through referral by the House of Representatives (1) from a member of the House or (2) by suggestion of the Joint Committee on Internal Revenue and Taxation (this is a committee of 10 members—five from the House Ways and Means Committee and five from the Senate Finance Committee).

- The Ways and Means Committee conducts hearings on the revenue bill. Expert opinion will be heard that may influence the form and meaning of the statute.
- The Ways and Means Committee sends an amended bill with the committee's report to the House for adoption.
- The adopted bill is sent to the Senate.
- The Senate sends the bill to the Senate Finance Committee where it is studied, hearings on it are held, and amendments to the bill are made. The amended bill and the committee report are then forwarded to the Senate for passage.
- Sometimes—where there are material differences between the House's version of the bill and the Senate's—a joint conference committee consisting of members from both sides develops a compromise version.
- The compromise version must be passed by both houses of the Congress.
- The bill is sent to the president for his signature or veto.
- If the president vetoes the bill, a two-thirds majority of both houses can revise the bill and make it law over the president's veto.

Once a law becomes effective, all taxpayers must follow it unless the law is declared unconstitutional. For example, a law taxing the income of men and women at different rates would be unconstitutional.

Once effective, the law is subject to a great deal of interpretation. The House Ways and Means Committee and the Senate Finance Committee reports become extremely important. Both the courts and the Department of Treasury Regulations (discussed below) rely heavily on these reports to determine the intent of the creators before an interpretation is made.

The Code itself contains seven subtitles. Subtitle A is concerned with income taxes; Subtitle B is concerned with estate and gift taxes; and the rest are concerned with other areas of taxation. The Code is then further subdivided. Each subtitle consists of chapters, subchapters, parts, subparts, sections, subsections, paragraphs, subparagraphs, and subparagraph subdivisions known as clauses.

Executive

The president, as the chief enforcer of the law under Article II of the Constitution, has the duty to enforce the collection of tax. He has delegated his responsibility to the Department of the Treasury that, in turn, has delegated the responsibility to its subdivision, the Internal Revenue Service.

The Department of the Treasury has also been granted the power by Congress to enact regulations under the Code. Congress, recognizing that the Code must be written in legal language but that it would not be the proper place to explain how the law will be applied to specific taxpayers, empowered the secretary of the Treasury or his or her delegate to promulgate the rules and regulations that are necessary to enforce the law. Thus the Code itself provides for the Treasury Department to prescribe the rules and regulations needed for the enforcement of the Code. Actually, the Internal Revenue Service writes these regulations, and the secretary of the Treasury approves them. Regulations are issued first in proposed form so that interested taxpayers may file objections or participate in public hearings before the proposed regulations are finalized.

The regulations, or "regs" as they are often called, constitute the official Treasury interpretation of the Code. Regulations may particularize, define, clarify, illustrate, or even amplify the Code. To the extent that these regs are not inconsistent with the Code, they are said to have the force and effect of law. Generally they are presumed to be correct, are followed by Treasury personnel, and are seldom invalidated by the courts. Because they are carefully prepared and unlikely to be quickly changed, taxpayers can ordinarily rely on them in everyday transactions.

Regulations can be held invalid by the courts for a number of reasons. The two principal ones are (1) the regulation is ambiguous and without persuasive force in determining the true construction of a statute, and (2) the regulation goes beyond the statute (the Code) and thus has no effect. Even if a regulation is held invalid by a lower court, the Treasury can still continue to enforce it unless the Supreme Court itself holds the regulation invalid.

Thus the IRS does not consider itself bound (beyond that particular case) where a regulation is held invalid by any court lower than the Supreme Court, although it now conforms to circuit court decisions for the taxpayer's circuit. At times, therefore, the Service will continue to enforce a regulation (held invalid in a given case) against other taxpayers (even in almost identical circumstances) until the issue is decided by the Supreme Court itself.

The regulations can be accessed in a manner similar to the Code. For example, the regulations pertaining to Section 303 of the Code would use the number 303. Income tax regulations are preceded by the number 1 (one). Therefore the regulations pertaining to Code Section 303, "Distributions in Redemption of Stock to Pay Death Taxes," could be found under the number 1.303 of the regulations.

Revenue Rulings and Private Rulings

It would be impossible for the Code and regulations to cover the tax consequences of every possible factual situation that can arise. Frequently taxpayers request the Internal Revenue Service's view on the interpretation of a doubtful point of law. In response to these requests, the Service issues various types of administrative rulings.

Revenue rulings are based on a stated set of facts that usually involve a problem common to a number of taxpayers. These pronouncements are binding on officials of the IRS, and they follow them in their handling of issues arising in particular cases. For example, suppose the law is unclear as to whether a taxpayer can deduct the cost of moving a pet under the moving-expense deduction. If the Internal Revenue Service issues a revenue ruling to the effect that the cost of moving a pet is not deductible, all revenue agents will adhere to the ruling. The taxpayer has the choice of (1) relying upon rulings if the facts and circumstances are substantially the same or (2) challenging rulings in the courts. Unlike Treasury regulations, the courts need not give rulings any weight.

Revenue rulings are published in a weekly bulletin called the Internal Revenue Bulletin. They can be found in the following manner. The first number following the abbreviation "Rev. Rul." gives the year the ruling was issued. This is followed by a dash. The second number is in numerical sequence, denoting the order in which the ruling was issued. Rev. Rul. 64-19 would be a ruling issued in 1964 and the 19th such revenue ruling issued in that year. The citation in the Internal Revenue Bulletin would include (1) the year, (2) the number of the weekly bulletin of that year, and (3) the page under which the ruling could be found. For example, Rev. Rul. 69-173, IRB 1969-15, 12, means that the particular ruling in 1969 was the 173rd of that year. It would be found in the 15th weekly bulletin issued in 1969 on page 12.

Private rulings arise when a taxpayer requests an administrative interpretation on a prospective transaction or on completed transactions that are not involved in returns already filed. Although private rulings are personal to the taxpayer, they have been made available to the public in recent years and are now published after the deletion of certain information. Deleted materials include names and addresses of taxpayers, trade secrets, classified matter, and so forth. Even though published, they still have the same effect—they may not be claimed by another taxpayer as a precedent.

Revenue Procedures

Revenue procedures describe internal practices and procedures within the IRS. Like revenue rulings, they are published in the Internal Revenue Bulletin. Generally revenue procedures state changes in techniques and administrative procedures used by the Internal Revenue Service. Revenue procedures are generally designated by the abbreviation "Rev. Proc."

Determination Letters

The Internal Revenue Service has three tiers: (1) the Washington, D.C., national headquarters, (2) the regions, and (3) the districts. The national office issues revenue rulings. District directors have the power to write determination letters regarding completed transactions[1] to be reflected on returns that will be filed in their respective districts. However, this occurs only if the answer to the question presented is covered specifically by statute, Treasury decision, or regulation, or specifically by a ruling opinion or court decision published in the Internal Revenue Bulletin. Determination letters contrast with revenue rulings in that such letters are never issued about unclear points of law.

Certain *key* district directors have the authority to issue determination letters relating to the exemption of charitable organizations and the qualification of pension trusts under Section 401 of the Internal Revenue Code.

Conflict between Taxpayers and the Internal Revenue Service

Individual taxpayers must file returns by April 15 for the previous calendar year or, if they are fiscal taxpayers, by the 15th day of the 4th month after their fiscal year ends. Corporations must file tax returns by March 15, or the 15th day of the 3d month after their fiscal year ends.

Once a return is filed, the Internal Revenue Service processes the form for mathematical accuracy and audit selection at its service center. The IRS has 3 years from the time the return was filed within which to assess additional taxes. Early returns are deemed to be filed on their due date. An important exception to the 3-year statute of limitations exists when fraud is involved. In this situation, there is unlimited time to audit.

An initial audit by an IRS examiner may take place at an IRS office or at the taxpayer's home or business. A preliminary letter advising the taxpayer of the agent's recommendation and a 30-day right to appeal from that determination will then be sent. If the taxpayer disagrees with the conclusion, he or she may write to the district director requesting a hearing before an appeals office of the Regional Appellate Division.

While the case is pending with the appeals officers, the taxpayer has the right to request that the issue be referred to the national office for technical advice. Grounds for referral to Washington are either that there has been a lack of uniformity in the disposition of the issue or that the complexity or uniqueness of the issue warrants consideration by the national office.

If no agreement can be reached with the Appellate Division, statutory notice of deficiency is issued by the commissioner of Internal Revenue. Following this notice, taxpayers have 90 days to file a petition with the U.S. Tax Court to have their cases heard. If taxpayers allow the 90 days to pass without either paying the tax and/or instituting suit, the IRS can assess a tax deficiency, enter judgment, and seize the taxpayers' property to collect the deficiency.

No tax need be paid in advance for cases to be litigated in the U.S. Tax Court. Once a case has been docketed there, an appeals officer is assigned to the case and given exclusive authority to settle within a 4-month period. If no settlement is reached in that time, the case is scheduled for trial.

Alternatively, the taxpayer may choose to pay the tax deficiency and then file a claim for a refund with the district director's office. Unless a notice of claim disallowance is sent before 6 months expire, the taxpayer must wait that time period before he or she can file suit for a refund in either the U.S. District Court or the U.S. Court of Federal Claims. Various factors discussed below will affect the taxpayer's choice of the best tribunal before which to try the case. By statute, the taxpayer has 2 years from the date the notice of the claim disallowance was mailed in which to sue the government for a refund. This 2-year period may be extended only by a written agreement between the taxpayer and the secretary of the Treasury. The income tax appeal procedure is illustrated on page 15.

Judicial

Article III of the U.S. Constitution states that judicial power shall be vested in one Supreme Court and in such lower courts as Congress shall establish. The jurisdiction of the federal courts includes all cases arising under the laws of the United States, including revenue laws.

The court system that Congress has established comprises trial courts that decide issues of fact and law, appellate courts for a review of issues of law, and the Supreme Court, which is the ultimate reviewer of questions of law.

U.S. Tax Court

The U.S. Tax Court was established for taxpayers who seek a redetermination of a deficiency asserted against them but do not wish first to pay the deficiency. A large majority of tax cases are heard by the Tax Court for this reason. Trial by jury is not available in the Tax Court. Questions of law and fact are decided by Tax Court judges.

The Tax Court has its main offices and trial rooms in Washington, D.C., but trials are conducted also in principal cities throughout the United States. The Tax Court is a special court designed principally for taxpayers who appeal tax deficiencies imposed by the Treasury Department.

Income Tax Appeal Procedure

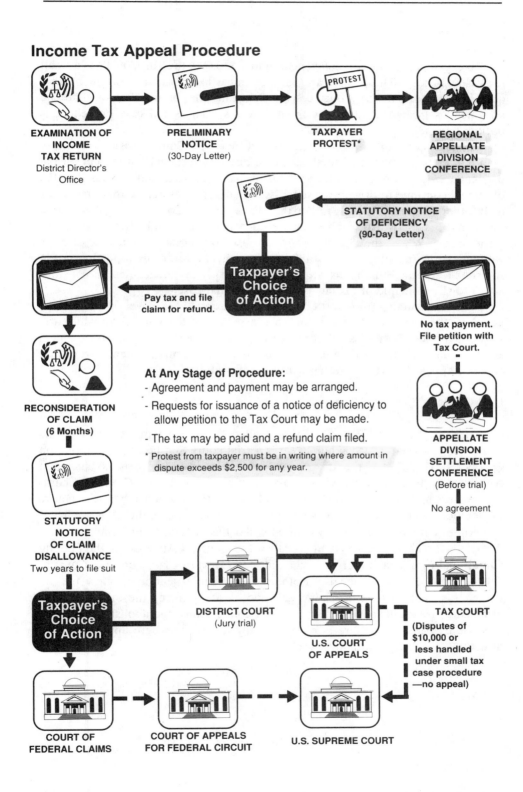

EXAMINATION OF INCOME TAX RETURN
District Director's Office

PRELIMINARY NOTICE
(30-Day Letter)

TAXPAYER PROTEST*

REGIONAL APPELLATE DIVISION CONFERENCE

STATUTORY NOTICE OF DEFICIENCY
(90-Day Letter)

Taxpayer's Choice of Action

Pay tax and file claim for refund.

No tax payment. File petition with Tax Court.

RECONSIDERATION OF CLAIM
(6 Months)

At Any Stage of Procedure:
- Agreement and payment may be arranged.
- Requests for issuance of a notice of deficiency to allow petition to the Tax Court may be made.
- The tax may be paid and a refund claim filed.

* Protest from taxpayer must be in writing where amount in dispute exceeds $2,500 for any year.

APPELLATE DIVISION SETTLEMENT CONFERENCE
(Before trial)

No agreement

STATUTORY NOTICE OF CLAIM DISALLOWANCE
Two years to file suit

Taxpayer's Choice of Action

DISTRICT COURT
(Jury trial)

U.S. COURT OF APPEALS

TAX COURT
(Disputes of $10,000 or less handled under small tax case procedure —no appeal)

COURT OF FEDERAL CLAIMS

COURT OF APPEALS FOR FEDERAL CIRCUIT

U.S. SUPREME COURT

To expedite hearings on deficiencies under $10,000, the Tax Court has a small tax case division. These cases are handled much less formally and much more quickly than formal Tax Court cases. Decisions of this division may not be appealed or treated as authority in other cases. The small case procedure is optional at the taxpayer's request.

The IRS does not consider itself bound by a Tax Court decision any more than it does by a Court of Federal Claims or district court decision (except for the particular case in which an adverse decision has been rendered). Thus the IRS often will continue to litigate the same issue in other cases before the same court or in other courts. However, rather than have the Tax Court rule against it in a number of cases (which establishes precedent), the IRS will often negotiate a settlement. When the Service loses a Tax Court case, it will indicate its willingness or unwillingness to follow the case in the future by reporting in the Internal Revenue Bulletin its acquiescence ("acq.") or nonacquiescence ("non-acq.") to the principle of tax law established in that case.

Appeals from the Tax Court either by an unsuccessful taxpayer or the IRS are heard by the U.S. Court of Appeals in the region of the country in which the taxpayer resides. If there is a difference of opinion in the various courts of appeal as to the interpretation of the tax law, the Tax Court follows the decisions of that court of appeals to which the taxpayer may appeal.

U.S. Court of Federal Claims

The U.S. Court of Federal Claims (called the U.S. Claims Court until its name was changed in December 1992) is a trial court that became operative on October 1, 1982, when the U.S. Court of Claims ceased to exist as such. It continues to hear cases that would have been heard by the old Court of Claims whose jurisdiction was limited to refund cases (the tax must be paid before jurisdiction can be invoked). Appeals from the Court of Federal Claims are heard by another court simultaneously created under the Federal Courts Improvement Act of 1982. This appellate court is called the Court of Appeals for the Federal Circuit and is, in fact, a merger of the old U.S. Court of Claims and the Court of Customs and Patents Appeals. Both of these courts generally follow the tax precedents of the Court of Claims as opposed to following the tax precedents established by the taxpayer's home district court. Since the abolishment of the U.S. Court of Claims, there is no longer any tax forum where appeal is taken directly to the U.S. Supreme Court.

U.S. District Court

The U.S. District Court (of which there is at least one for each state) like the U.S. Court of Federal Claims can only hear tax cases in which the taxpayer has first paid the deficiency and has been denied a refund by the Internal Revenue Service.

The U.S. District Court is unique in that it is the only court in which a taxpayer may request a jury trial. In a case where there is a jury, the jury decides questions of fact; the judge decides questions of law. For example, sometimes the taxpayers will choose to institute suit in a district court because their battles with the IRS are essentially factual, and they believe they will obtain a sympathetic jury. As to questions of law, a district court in a certain location must follow decisions of that particular court's corresponding court of appeals as precedent. Appeals from a district court can be made to the U.S. Court of Appeals and then further to the Supreme Court.

U.S. Court of Appeals

The U.S. Court of Appeals comprises 12 circuit courts located throughout the country. These courts hear appeals that are taken by either taxpayers or the Treasury from decisions rendered by the Tax Court or a district court. The U.S. Court of Appeals is the second highest level in the court system. The importance of this court is underscored by the fact that the only appeal from a decision of such a court is to the Supreme Court itself. Both the district courts and the Tax Court must follow decisions of the Court of Appeals to which the taxpayer may appeal. The court of appeals of one region is not bound to follow decisions by the court of appeals in another region. Although a favorable decision in a sister court may be persuasive, it is not controlling. Taxpayers who must use the court of appeals in a region other than where the favorable decision was rendered cannot be sure of the outcome of their cases, even if the facts of their cases are almost identical to the facts of the case previously decided elsewhere. Of course, a favorable decision in one circuit may be relied upon by other taxpayers in that same circuit.

U.S. Supreme Court

The United States Supreme Court is the highest court in the land. Supreme Court decisions are required to be followed by taxpayers as well as by the Internal Revenue Service. However, there are few tax cases that the high court decides. This is because Supreme Court review of tax cases is generally available only if the Court itself grants petitions for appeal. Supreme Court review, therefore, is a matter of discretion with the Supreme Court and not a matter of right. The

Supreme Court will most probably review a tax case if (1) there is a conflict between the courts of appeal for different circuits, or (2) an important and recurring problem in tax law administration is involved, or (3) many taxpayers are involved, or (4) the decision of a lower court conflicts with long-standing practice or the regulations.

A Supreme Court interpretation of tax law is the law of the land until (1) Congress enacts a new statute, tantamount to overturning a decision interpreting the Internal Revenue Code, or (2) the Court overrides its own prior decision in rare situations.

SUMMARY

The history of the income tax parallels the history of the financial needs of the United States. The strain of a modern government attempting to meet the costs of both wartime expenditures and peacetime services created a demand for additional revenues. Once established, the overriding importance of the individual and corporate income taxes in the federal revenue structure has never diminished.

Aside from revenue purposes, the income tax has been used with varying degrees of success to perform social, economic, and regulatory functions.

The source of the federal income tax law is ultimately the people. The intent of the people was expressed through the Constitution, which in turn gives legislative power to Congress. Congress exercises this power in the form of the Internal Revenue Code, which is further modified and expanded by the Internal Revenue Service's regulations and rulings. Court decisions on particular issues further interpret and expound on statutory law as well as IRS regulations and rulings. The importance and effect of these court cases is in turn determined by the status of the court. The hierarchy of the court system (and hence the weight given to a decision of that particular court) at the highest level starts with the Supreme Court and works its way down to courts of original jurisdiction known as the United States Court of Federal Claims, the United States District Court, and the United States Tax Court.

NOTE

1. An exception to this rule occurs where a taxpayer seeks an advance-determination letter to qualify an employee retirement plan for tax benefits prior to the actual installation of the plan.

3

What the Financial Services Professional Should Know about the Doctrine of Constructive Receipt and Economic Benefit Theory

Stephan R. Leimberg and Stephen N. Kandell[*]

Two of the most important tax law concepts are the doctrine of constructive receipt and the economic benefit theory. The purpose of this discussion is to give the financial services professional a working knowledge of how these principles work as well as to examine specifically their application to life insurance products and services. Although both the doctrine of constructive receipt and the economic benefit theory are used to explain why a taxpayer should be currently taxable on income, there are important distinctions that will be considered shortly.

The doctrine of constructive receipt will be considered first. The doctrine will be defined, its purpose and operation in typical situations will be described, and its effect on life insurance products and services will be studied. The economic benefit theory will then be discussed and distinguished from the doctrine of constructive receipt. In order to highlight some of the basic issues involved in this area, a question and answer format will be used.

Question: What is the doctrine of constructive receipt?

Answer: Before answering that question directly, it is necessary to review what is meant by the *cash receipts and disbursements* or *cash-basis* method of accounting. Most financial services professionals and their clients are cash-basis taxpayers, which means that they report income and pay taxes on that income only if it is received during the taxable year. Almost all individual taxpayers who are

---

*Stephen N. Kandell is director of estate and business analysis at Consolidated Brokerage Services, Inc., Conshohocken, Pennsylvania.

not in a trade or business (and many who are in a trade or business) use this method of accounting.

For example, suppose your client—a doctor on the cash-basis method of accounting—renders services but is not paid for them until January of next year. The income will not be includible in the doctor's income for this year but will be reportable next year, even though the services were performed this year.

In a nutshell, the cash-basis method of accounting means that an individual reports income in the year it is received. More formally stated, the amount of any item of gross income shall be included in the gross income of the taxpayer for the taxable year in which it is received, unless an accounting method is used in which such income is to be properly accounted for as of a different period.

Question: Generally, then, a cash-basis taxpayer does not have to report income until and unless this person actually receives it. How does the doctrine of constructive receipt apply to this general rule?

Answer: There is an exception to the general rule that income is reported by a cash-basis taxpayer only when it is actually received. The exception is known as the theory or doctrine of constructive receipt. This doctrine might best be illustrated by restating two questions often asked of financial services professionals:

1. Is the interest earned on life insurance policy dividend accumulations currently taxable to the policyholder at the time it is credited to the policyholder's account, even though the interest is not actually received by the policyholder at that time?
2. If a policyholder takes the maturity proceeds or cash surrender value of the life, endowment, or annuity contract in the form of a life income or in installments (rather than as a lump sum), is the entire gain on the policy taxable to him or her in the year of maturity or surrender?

Question: What is the problem? It is evident that in either case the policyholder does not have actual receipt of income.

Answer: In both situations above, the policyholder might have received income *constructively,* even though he or she has not actually reduced income to his or her possession. The problem is caused by a section of the income tax regulations that provides that income must be included in the taxpayer's gross income for the taxable year in which it is "actually or constructively received." This means that a taxpayer does not have to reduce income to actual possession before it has to be reported. An individual must report it as soon as it is either (1) actually received or (2) constructively received.

Regulations elaborate by stating that even though income is not actually reduced to a taxpayer's possession, the taxpayer is deemed to have constructively received it in the taxable year during which (1) it is credited to the taxpayer's account, (2) set apart for the taxpayer, or (3) otherwise made available to be drawn upon at any time.

Question: These rules seem very strict. Are there exceptions?

Answer: The regulations qualify the constructive receipt rules by stating that income is *not* constructively received if the taxpayer's control of its receipt is subject to substantial limitations or restrictions. In essence, therefore, the implications of these regulations to cash-basis life underwriters and their cash-basis policyholders is that they must report currently any income that has become unconditionally subject to their demand, although in fact they have not chosen to actually receive or reduce that income to their possession.

You might think of the doctrine of constructive receipt as being the "Can I get it when I want it?" doctrine. When taxpayers decide to actually obtain items of income and only their volition stands between them and the income, they have constructively received the income at that time (and are therefore taxed on it).

Question: What is the reason for the doctrine?

Answer: The purpose of the constructive receipt rules is to prevent taxpayers from unilaterally determining the tax year when an item of income is "received by" them for federal income tax purposes. Were it not for this doctrine, cash-basis taxpayers could shift, at will, the year in which they will report an item of income, merely by taking no steps to reduce that income to their possession. The rule prevents cash-basis taxpayers from avoiding taxes by putting off actual receipt of income until their tax circumstances are more favorable, tax rates are lower, or they have a lower amount of other includible income.

The thrust of the doctrine of constructive receipt may therefore be capsulized by the statement that a cash-basis taxpayer "may not deliberately turn his back upon income and thus select the year for which he will report it." If income is payable on the demand of a taxpayer in a given taxable year, he or she must include such amounts in his or her taxable income for that year. To hold otherwise would permit a taxpayer to defer taxable income by merely choosing not to exercise the right to receive it. Therefore the owner of a savings account cannot defer the year in which interest earnings must be reported by deciding in December not to walk into a bank and have that interest credited on his or her passbook until the following January.

Question: What is the effect when there are substantial limitations or restrictions placed on a taxpayer's right to receive income?

Answer: The regulations qualify the rules on inclusion of constructively received income by stating that income will not be constructively received if the taxpayer's control of its receipt is subject to substantial limitations or substantial restrictions. For example, suppose Lee, a pension consultant, signs a contract to perform actuarial services during this year. Lee actually performs those services during this year. However, the contract specifies that payment will not be made until 5 years from now. Lee has no right to require earlier payment. Because payment to Lee (a cash-basis taxpayer) was subject to a substantial restriction (that is, it was not payable until 5 years later), it should not be considered constructively received this year. Thus where a taxpayer is not legally entitled to receive payment in a year prior to actual receipt, this individual will not be held to have constructively received that income in the prior year.

This raises the central question of whether the taxpayer merely refrained from exercising a legal right to receive current payment or whether there was actually never a legal right to receive payment in the prior year. The answer is a question of fact that will be determined by examining the agreement between the parties in each situation. Court cases indicate that if there is any substantial limitation or restriction on either the time or the manner of payment of income, there can be no constructive receipt until the limitation or restriction is removed. There would be no constructive receipt, for example, if the Tyler Corporation raises the salary of Robert, but does not pay that salary increase until a later year when wage freeze rules are changed to permit payment. Robert will not be deemed to be in constructive receipt in the earlier year.

Question: How does the effect of substantial limitations or restrictions apply to life insurance?

Answer: The cash value of a life insurance policy earns interest, which is reflected in the increase in the policy cash value from year to year. Although a policyholder could easily reduce any gain reflected by the excess of the cash value over the cost of the contract, the policyholder is not required to include such gain in his or her gross income each year. This is because the right to receive that income is subject to substantial limitations or restrictions; that is, to receive the gain the policyholder must complete a transaction that will affect the nature and extent of his or her valuable insurance coverage and contractual rights.

Question: Suppose amounts are credited or set apart for a taxpayer, but there are no funds to pay the promised amounts. What is the effect on an inability to pay amounts credited?

Answer: If the financial condition of the debtor makes payment of the income in question impossible, there will be no constructive receipt by the creditor. For example, suppose Pam loaned the Strand Corporation $10,000. In return Pam received an interest-bearing note. If the Strand Corporation had insufficient funds to pay the interest, Pam would have no constructive receipt even if her account was credited with the interest on the corporation's books. Likewise, if the Martin Corporation issued a salary check to Oliver, an officer, but the corporation lacked the funds to pay the check, Oliver would not be taxed. This result would hold even if the Martin Corporation could have borrowed money or sold assets to pay the check.

Question: Specifically, how does the doctrine of constructive receipt affect life insurance?

Answer: At this point it is appropriate to answer the two questions asked earlier:

1. Is the interest earned on life insurance policy dividend accumulations currently taxable to the policyholder as soon as it is credited to the policyholder's account, even if the policyholder has not actually received the interest?
2. If a policyholder takes the maturity proceeds or cash surrender value of the life, endowment, or annuity contract in the form of a life income or in installments (rather than in a lump sum), is the gain on the policy taxable to him or her in the year of maturity or surrender?

The first question pertains to the time at which interest earned on policy dividends becomes taxable. The general rule is that the interest earned on policy dividends must be included in the policyholder's gross income for the first taxable year during which the policyholder has the right to withdraw the interest. This result applies even if the taxpayer, in fact, does not withdraw the interest. The key issue is the following: When can the policyholder withdraw the interest on the policy dividends? If the policy provides that interest can be withdrawn only on the policy anniversary date, the interest income is not constructively received in the year prior to the anniversary date.

The second question pertains to the result that occurs when the maturity proceeds or cash surrender value of a policy are taken in the form of installments of lifetime payments rather than in the form of a lump sum. When an endowment contract matures (or an ordinary life contract is surrendered), gain on the lump sum available to the policyholder will be immediately taxable. However, if a policyholder decides to select an installment payment or annuity settlement option, rather than taking the lump sum that could be chosen at will, is the policyholder in constructive receipt of the lump sum? If there is a gain on the contract and if proceeds are constructively received, the full gain would be taxable—just as if the policyholder had actually received a lump-sum payment.

A constructive receipt problem can occur in three typical situations. The first situation is when the policyholder elects *before* the maturity or surrender date to postpone receipt of the proceeds and take income in the form of an annuity or installments. In this case, however, the policyholder avoids constructive receipt since there is no point in time when he or she had an unqualified right to take the lump sum. The policyholder will be taxed on the gain reflected in each installment when he or she actually receives it.

The second situation is when a policyholder does *not* make an election before the maturity or surrender date. Were it not for special provision in the Internal Revenue Code, the policyholder would be considered to be in constructive receipt of the lump sum when it became available. However, because of this special provision, a policyholder will not be deemed to be in constructive receipt of the lump sum (1) within 60 days after the lump sum becomes payable and (2) if before receiving any payment in cash, the policyholder exercises an option or agrees with the insurer to take the proceeds in the form of a life income annuity or other installment-type settlement.

The third situation occurs when a policyholder decides to give up the right to withdraw principal, leaves proceeds on deposit, and receives only the interest that those proceeds generate. Constructive receipt in this case can be avoided only if an election to receive interest is made *before* the maturity or surrender date. Thus the 60-day extension is allowed only for the election of a life income or other installment-type settlement and not for an election to leave proceeds on deposit at interest.

Question: Does the doctrine of constructive receipt affect agreements to defer compensation?

Answer: It is in the area of deferred compensation that the doctrine of constructive receipt proves to be most complex and troublesome. The reason for deferring compensation is quite simple: If all or a part of an individual's current earnings are not payable by an employer until a specified date, or if those earnings are spread out over a number of years in the future when the individual is in a lower income tax bracket, the net aftertax compensation will be increased. Therefore it is possible to defer the tax of a cash-basis employee or independent contractor, but this deferral requires careful planning.

Basically there are two types of deferred-compensation methods: (1) funded and (2) unfunded. A funded deferred-compensation agreement entails the actual deposit of funds by the employer into a trust, escrow, or custodial account. Unfunded deferred compensation implies that no funds are irrevocably set aside (that is, outside the corporation's control and beyond the reach of its creditors) by an employer. In this case, the employee must rely solely on the employer's unsecured promise and ability to pay the deferred amount (plus any interest that is applicable) in the future. Taxation generally depends not only on whether the agreement is funded or unfunded but also on whether the rights of the employee whose income is deferred are forfeitable or nonforfeitable.

Where the agreement can be classified as funded (according to the definition above), the deferred compensation will be taxable to the employee in (a) the first year the employee's rights are not subject to a substantial risk of forfeiture, or (b) the first year the employee's rights can be transferred to another party (that is, assigned free of the substantial risk of forfeiture).

If the agreement can be classified as unfunded (according to the definition above), such compensation will not be taxable until it is actually paid to the employee provided (a) the agreement to defer the compensation is made *prior* to the time the compensation is earned, and (b) the employer's promise is not secured by specific assets. In other words, the obligation may not be evidenced by specified financial instruments, such as a negotiable note. If these two requirements are met, constructive receipt will be avoided until the deferred compensation is actually received. This is because receipt of the compensation is not within the employee's control. This result will apply regardless of whether such compensation was or was not forfeitable by the employee. Therefore even if the employee had a nonforfeitable right to such compensation, no tax would be imposed until actual receipt since the agreement was unfunded.

For example, suppose in order to entice Elaine to join the Rawlins Corporation Elaine was offered a 5-year employment contract. The agreement provides that Elaine will be paid $50,000 a year currently, plus an additional $10,000 of nonforfeitable deferred compensation credited to a reserve account each year. However, Elaine will receive the money only upon her retirement, death, or disability. Elaine receives neither notes from the corporation nor evidence of its debt other than the agreement signed by the corporation and Elaine. She is to receive the deferred salary in 10 equal annual installments.

Even though the compensation that has been deferred is nonforfeitable, Elaine does not have constructive receipt. The agreement to defer the compensation was made before Elaine earned it. The Rawlins Corporation did not put aside funds in an escrow account for her benefit. In no way did the Rawlins Corporation secure its promise to Elaine other than through an employment agreement. Thus she has no right to the funds. They have not been credited or set apart so that she may draw upon them at will. Therefore Elaine has merely a promise by the Rawlins Corporation to be paid income upon her retirement, death, or disability. Nothing has been placed beyond the access of the corporation's creditors, and no control over the funds has been given to Elaine. Likewise, upon retirement, death, or disability, when the Rawlins Corporation's promise matures and Elaine becomes entitled to receive installment payments, there is still no constructive receipt. The only income subject to her unqualified control is the installment payment she actually receives each year. These payments, of course, will be taxable income when actually paid to Elaine.

In recent years the Internal Revenue Service has allowed the use of *rabbi trusts* in connection with deferred-compensation agreements without imposing current taxation on the funds placed in the trust to be paid later to the employee. The employee will escape current taxation only if the funds in the trust can be reached by the creditors of the employer and if the deferred-compensation agreement does not require that a *specific* asset (such as a particular life insurance policy) be maintained in the trust to fund the agreement. The rabbi trust has been a significant development in terms of how the IRS regards the doctrine of constructive receipt, since it involves setting aside funds for the payment of deferred compensation without the arrangement being treated as a "funded" agreement.

Question: How is the use of life insurance in deferred-compensation agreements affected by the doctrine of constructive receipt?

Answer: Life insurance or annuity policies are often used by an employer to finance its obligation under the deferred-compensation agreement. For example, suppose the Mitchell Corporation executed a deferred-compensation contract with Sam, a key employee. The agreement stated that Mitchell would credit a specific sum on behalf of Sam to a bookkeeping account each month for the entire term of the contract. (This agreement is unfunded, since no amounts are set aside in trust or in an escrow account beyond the reach of the corporation's creditors.)

Mitchell could invest all or any portion of the amount credited to Sam. Payout would not commence until the earlier of (a) Sam's 65th birthday, (b) his death prior to retirement, or (c) his disability. At that time the value of the account would be paid out in equal installments over a period of 10 years to the employee or to his named beneficiary. To finance this liability under the agreement, Mitchell purchased a life insurance contract. Mitchell applied for, owned, and was beneficiary of the contract. The policy was carried as a corporate asset on the Mitchell Corporation books and was subject at all times to the claims of its general creditors.

The employee under this type of deferred-compensation contract will be successful in avoiding constructive receipt of the money set aside. The employee will recognize no income until the taxable year in which the income is actually received (or it is made available to the employee in some other way). The rationale is that the employee has no present interest in either the account or the policy, both of which are general assets of the employer. Note that the agreement gave the employee or his or her beneficiary no direct interest in any specific account, insurance or annuity policy, or in any other employer assets. The account merely served as a measure of the employer's liability for bookkeeping purposes.

Question: What is the economic benefit (cash equivalency) theory?

Answer: Sec. 61 of the Internal Revenue Code defines gross income as including "income from whatever source derived . . ." In cases dealing with this section of the Code, courts have held that the language of the section is "broad enough to include as taxable income any economic or financial benefit conferred on the employee as compensation, whatever the form or mode by which it is effected." This concept has appropriately been entitled the *economic benefit theory* or *doctrine.* Its purpose is to force an employee to include in income any compensation regardless of its form. It has been applied to situations involving a *payment in kind* or where an employer has made available to an employee the *equivalent of cash.*

Question: How does this principle differ from the doctrine of constructive receipt?

Answer: The constructive receipt doctrine forces the inclusion of income when the employee has an unqualified choice—to take or not to take income set apart or credited to his or her account. The economic benefit theory or doctrine, on the other hand, forces the inclusion of income, even if the employee *cannot* take the income. All that is necessary under the economic benefit theory is that the employee receive from an employer the equivalent of cash, something with a (a) current, (b) real, and (c) measurable value.

For example, if Pete is given the right to receive his bonus in cash or in the form of a nontransferable annuity with no cash values, he has constructive receipt of the bonus regardless of the choice he makes. The reason is that he has the unrestricted right to take the cash. Alternatively, if Pete was given no choice as to the form of his bonus—if it was only available to him in the form of a nontransferable, single-premium deferred annuity with no cash value—he would not have constructively received his bonus. This is because he can neither take cash nor draw down cash values from the annuity. Still, he would realize current income. He has received the promise of an insurance company, a financial institution in the business of making such promises, that he will receive benefits (his bonus) in the future.

The second situation illustrates the economic benefit theory. The secured promise of an insurance company or banking company to pay income in the future can be currently and adequately valued and is therefore immediately taxable. This is unlike the naked promise of an employer that is, in effect, a nonnegotiable, nonassignable agreement generally incapable of valuation, because the employer's promise is subject, according to the courts, to the hazards of economic and business conditions, regardless of the size or financial condition of the employer.

Perhaps the following case will illustrate further the distinction between the doctrine of constructive receipt and the economic benefit theory. An employer established a trust in 1945 for the benefit of one of his key employees. The employer placed $10,500 in the trust that year. The trustee was directed to pay that employee $5,000 in 1946 and the balance in 1947. In other words, the deferred compensation was irrevocably set aside in a trust and payable over a 2-year period. The court held that in 1945 the amount of $10,500 was fixed and irrevocably paid out by the employer for the sole benefit of the taxpayer. The court recognized that the employee technically had neither actual nor constructive receipt of the trust money. During 1945 he had no right whatsoever to draw upon those funds. Therefore the court reasoned that there was a substantial limitation on the employee's control, preventing constructive receipt. However, the court concluded that the employee did have an *actual receipt of the economic of financial benefit* conferred upon him in 1945. This was the year in which the employer established the irrevocable trust for the employee's benefit in which the employee's rights were nonforfeitable. In such a case, the employee would pay tax on the present value (1945 value) of the right to receive $5,000 one year later (1946), and an additional $5,500 two years later (1947).

Even though the funds were not immediately subject to his actual expenditure, they were there solely for his benefit. Therefore the amount of income he is to realize in the year in which the funds were set apart for his benefit must be measured by the amount of money paid, appropriately discounted to reflect the postponement of possession or enjoyment. Even this discount would not be allowed if the funds were placed in an interest-bearing account on which the employee would ultimately receive the interest.

Question: How might the economic benefit theory be applied in a life insurance situation?

Answer: There are several life insurance-related situations in which the economic benefit theory is applied. One such situation is the taxation of employees covered under a qualified pension or profit-sharing plan that contains life insurance on their lives. Another situation is where an employee receives group insurance in excess of the excludible limit. Perhaps the clearest example can be found in the taxation of split-dollar life insurance. Split-dollar insurance is an arrangement, typically between an employer and an employee, whereby policy premiums, cash values, dividends, and death benefits may be split. The classic example is where the employer pays that part of the annual premium that equals the current year's increase in the cash value. The employee pays the balance of any premium. Death benefits will be apportioned so that the employer recovers the total outlay, while the employee's family receives any balance. There are several variations on this traditional arrangement that are currently being used.

The employee is taxed currently on the value of the economic benefit received from the employer's participation in the split-dollar agreement. The benefit in question is the current insurance protection available to the employee under the basic policy. The value of this benefit is measured by government tables that contain one-year term insurance rates, so-called P.S. 58 premium rates.

The employee is deemed to have received a currently taxable economic benefit measured by the premium cost that would have been incurred for the net protection at this individual's attained age. Government tables (P.S. 58 rates) are used to determine this term cost. Policy dividends used to purchase one-year term insurance under the fifth dividend option or applied to purchase insurance in which the employee has a nonforfeitable interest likewise constitute an economic benefit to the employee (just as if those dividends had been received in cash). The value of this benefit is the actual dollar amount of dividends so used or received. The total value of all such economic benefits is added. The employee may then subtract from the total value of the economic benefit received any premium contribution that the employee makes. Any remaining balance is taxable to the employee during the current year as ordinary income. This amount represents the entire economic benefit the employee has received.

Conclusion

Question: In summary, what is the difference between the doctrine of constructive receipt and the economic benefit theory?

Answer: The doctrine of constructive receipt is concerned with the problem of *"when* income is realized by the taxpayer." The economic benefit theory, on the other hand, pertains to the question, Has the taxpayer currently enjoyed a benefit from an employer that is capable of measurement and subject to tax? In other words, the economic benefit theory is concerned with *what* is income rather than *when* it is realized.

4

Income Taxation of Group Life Insurance*

Burton T. Beam, Jr.

The growth of group life insurance has been greatly influenced by the favorable income tax treatment afforded it under federal tax laws. This reading will discuss the effects of these tax laws on basic group term insurance, coverages that may be added to a basic group term insurance contract, and group life insurance with permanent benefits. A complete explanation of the federal income tax laws pertaining to group life insurance, as well as their interpretation by the Internal Revenue Service, would be lengthy and is beyond the scope of this reading. Consequently, this discussion will only highlight these laws.

GROUP TERM LIFE INSURANCE

Deductibility of Premiums

In general, employer contributions for an employee's group term insurance coverage are fully deductible to the employer under Sec. 162 of the Internal Revenue Code as an ordinary and necessary business expense as long as the overall compensation of the employee is reasonable. The reasonableness of compensation (which includes wages, salary, and other fringe benefits) is usually only a potential issue for the owners of small businesses or the stockholder-employees of closely held corporations. Any compensation that is determined by the Internal Revenue Service to be unreasonable may not be deducted by a firm for income tax purposes. In addition, the Internal Revenue Code does not allow a firm to take an income tax deduction for contributions (1) that are made on behalf of sole proprietors or partners under any circumstances or (2) that are made on behalf of stockholders, unless they are providing substantial services to the corporation. Finally, no deduction is allowed under Sec. 264 of the Internal Revenue Code if the employer is named as beneficiary.

Contributions by any individual employee are considered payments for personal life insurance and are not deductible for income tax purposes by that

---

*Excerpted from *Group Benefits: Basic Concepts and Alternatives*, 6th ed., by Burton T. Beam, Jr. (Bryn Mawr, Pa.: The American College, 1995). Burton T. Beam, Jr., MBA, CLU, ChFC, CPCU, is associate professor of insurance at The American College.

employee. Thus the amount of any payroll deductions authorized by an employee for group term insurance purposes will be included in the employee's taxable income.

Income Tax Liability of Employees

In the absence of tax laws to the contrary, the amount of any compensation for which an employer receives an income tax deduction (including the payment of group insurance premiums) represents taxable income to the employee. However, Sec. 79 of the Internal Revenue Code provides favorable tax treatment to employer contributions for life insurance that qualifies as group term insurance.

Sec. 79 Requirements

In order to qualify as group term insurance under Sec. 79, life insurance must meet the following conditions:

- It must provide a death benefit excludible from federal income tax.
- It must be provided to a group of employees. A group of employees is defined to include all employees of an employer. If all employees are not covered, membership must be determined on the basis of age, marital status, or factors relating to employment.
- It must be provided under a policy carried directly or indirectly by the employer. This includes (1) any policy for which the employer pays any part of the cost or (2) if the employer pays no part of the cost, any policy arranged by the employer if at least one employee is charged less than his or her cost (under Table I, discussed below) and at least one other employee is charged more than his or her cost. If no employee is charged more than the Table I cost, a policy is not group term insurance for purposes of Sec. 79. A policy is defined to include a master contract of a group of individual policies. The term *carried indirectly* refers to those situations where the employer is not the policyowner, but rather provides coverage to employees through master contracts issued to organizations such as negotiated trusteeships or multiple-employer trusts.
- The plan must be arranged in such a manner as to preclude individual selection of coverage amounts. However, it is acceptable to have alternative benefit schedules based on the amount an employee elects to contribute. Supplemental plans where an employee is given a choice, such

as either 1, 1 1/2, or 2 times salary, are considered to fall within this category.

All life insurance that qualifies under Sec. 79 as group term insurance is considered to be a single plan of insurance, regardless of the number of insurance contracts used. For example, an employer might provide coverage for union employees under a negotiated trusteeship, for other employees under an individual employer group insurance contract, and additional coverage for top executives under a group of individual life insurance policies. Under Sec. 79 these would all constitute a single plan. This plan must be provided for at least 10 full-time employees at some time during the calendar year. For purposes of meeting the 10-life requirement, employees who have not satisfied any required waiting periods may be counted as participants. In addition, employees who have elected not to participate are also counted as participants—but only if they would not have been required to contribute to the cost of other benefits besides group term insurance if they had participated. As will be described later, a plan with fewer than 10 full-time employees may still qualify for favorable tax treatment under Sec. 79 if more restrictive requirements are met.

Exceptions to Sec. 79

Even when all the previous requirements are met, there are some situations in which Sec. 79 does not apply. In some cases different sections of the Internal Revenue Code provide alternative tax treatment. For example, when group term insurance is issued to the trustees of a qualified pension plan and is used to provide a death benefit under the plan, the full amount of any life insurance paid for by employer contributions will result in taxable income to the employee.

There are three situations in which employer contributions for group term insurance will not result in taxable income to an employee, regardless of the amount of insurance: (1) if an employee has terminated employment because of disability; (2) if a qualified charity (as determined by the Internal Revenue Code) has been named as beneficiary for the entire period during the tax year for which the employee receives insurance; or (3) if the employer has been named as beneficiary for the entire year.

Coverage on retired employees is subject to Sec. 79, and these persons are treated in the same manner as active employees. Thus they will have taxable income in any year in which the amount of coverage received exceeds $50,000. However, a grandfather clause to this new rule stipulates that it does not apply to group term life insurance plans (or to comparable successor plans or to plans of successor employers) in existence on January 1, 1984, for covered employees who (1) retired before 1984 or (2) were at least 55 years of age before 1984 and were employed by the employer any time during 1983. There is one exception to this grandfather clause: it does not apply to persons retiring after 1986 if a plan is discriminatory.

General Tax Rules

Under Sec. 79 the cost of the first $50,000 of coverage is not taxed to the employee. Since all group term insurance that qualifies under Sec. 79 is considered to be one plan, this exclusion applies only once to each employee. For example, an employee who has $10,000 of coverage under a policy for all employees and $75,000 of coverage under a separate insurance policy for executives would have a single $50,000 exclusion. The cost of coverage in excess of $50,000, less any employee contributions for the entire amount of coverage, represents taxable income to the employee. For purposes of Sec. 79, the cost of this excess coverage is determined by a government table called the Uniform Premium Table I. This table will often result in a lower cost than would be calculated by using the actual premium paid by the employer for the coverage.

UNIFORM PREMIUM TABLE I	
Age	**Cost per Month per $1,000 of Coverage**
29 and under	$ .08
30–34	.09
35–39	.11
40–44	.17
45–49	.29
50–54	.48
55–59	.75
60–64	1.17
65–69	2.10
70 and over	3.76

To calculate the cost of an employee's coverage for one month of protection under a group term insurance plan, the Uniform Premium Table I cost shown for the employee's age bracket (based on the employee's attained age at the end of the tax year) is multiplied by the number of thousands in excess of 50 of group term insurance on the employee. For example, if an employee, aged 57, was provided with $150,000 of group term insurance, the employee's monthly cost (assuming no employee contributions) would be calculated as follows:

Coverage provided	$150,000
Less Sec. 79 exclusion	50,000
Amount subject to taxation	$100,000
Uniform Premium Table I monthly cost	
per $1,000 of coverage at age 57	$ 0.75
Monthly cost ($0.75 x 100)	$75.00

The monthly costs are then totaled to obtain an annual cost. Assuming no change in the amount of coverage during the year, the annual cost would be $900. Any employee contributions for the entire amount of coverage are subtracted from the annual cost to determine the taxable income that must be reported by an employee. If the employee contributed $.30 per month ($3.60 per year) per $1,000 of coverage, the employee's total annual contribution for $150,000 of coverage would be $540. This reduces the amount reportable as taxable income from $900 to $360.

It is important to note that group term insurance coverage can often be purchased at a lower cost than Table I rates. There are some who argue that, in these instances, the actual cost of coverage can be used in place of the Table I cost for determining an employee's taxable income. From the standpoint of logic and consistency with the tax laws, this view makes sense. However, the law clearly provides that Table I costs must be used.

Nondiscrimination Rules

Any plan that qualifies as group term insurance under Sec. 79 is subject to nondiscrimination rules, and the $50,000 exclusion will not be available to key employees if a plan is discriminatory. Such a plan might favor key employees in either eligibility or benefits. If the plan is discriminatory, the value of the full amount of coverage for key employees, less their own contributions, will be considered taxable income, based on the greater of actual or Table I costs. A key employee of a firm is defined as any person who at any time during the current plan year or the preceding 4 plan years is any of the following:

- an officer of the firm who earns from the firm more than 50 percent of the Internal Revenue Code limit on the amount of benefits payable by a defined-benefit plan. This amount (50 percent of $115,641, or $57,820.50 for 1993) is indexed annually. For purposes of this rule the number of employees treated as officers is the greater of 3 or 10 percent of the firm's employees, subject to a maximum of 50. In applying the rule certain employees can be excluded. These include persons who are part-time, under 21, or have less than 6 months of service with the firm.

- one of the 10 employees owning the largest interests in the firm and having an annual compensation from the firm of more than $30,000
- a more-than-5-percent owner of the firm
- a more-than-one-percent owner of the firm who earns over $150,000 per year
- a retired employee who was a key employee when he or she retired or terminated service

Note that the definition of key employee includes not only active employees but also retired employees who were key employees at the time of retirement or separation from service.

Eligibility requirements are not discriminatory if (1) at least 70 percent of all employees are eligible, (2) at least 85 percent of all employees who are participants are not key employees, or (3) participants comprise a classification that the IRS determines is nondiscriminatory. For purposes of the 70 percent test employees with less than 3 years' service, part-time employees, and seasonal employees may be excluded. Employees covered by collective-bargaining agreements may also be excluded if plan benefits were the subject of good-faith bargaining.

Benefits are not discriminatory if neither the type nor amount of benefits discriminates in favor of key employees. The act specifies that it is permissible to base benefits on a uniform percentage of salary.

One issue that arose after the passage of the nondiscrimination rules in 1984 was whether they applied separately to active and to retired employees. A technical correction in the Tax Reform Act of 1986 clarified the issued by stating that the rules do apply separately to the extent provided in IRS regulations. However, such regulations have yet to be issued.

Groups with Fewer than 10 Full-time Employees

A group insurance plan that covers fewer than 10 employees must also satisfy another set of nondiscrimination requirements before it is eligible for favorable tax treatment under Sec. 79. These requirements, which are set forth in Treasury regulations, make smaller groups subject to two separate and somewhat overlapping sets of rules.

It should again be noted that Sec. 79 applies to an employer's overall plan of group insurance, not to separate group insurance contracts. For example, an employer providing group insurance coverage for its 50 hourly employees under one group insurance contract and for its 6 executives under a separate contract is considered to have a single plan covering 56 employees, and thus is exempt from the under-10 requirements. While the stated purpose of the under-10 requirements is to preclude individual selection, their effect is to prevent the group insurance plan from discriminating in favor of the owners or stockholder-employees of small businesses.

With some exceptions, plans covering fewer than 10 employees must provide coverage for all full-time employees. For purposes of this requirement, employees who are not customarily employed for more than 20 hours in any one week or 5 months in any calendar year are considered part-time employees. It is permissible to exclude full-time employees from coverage under the following circumstances:

- The employee has reached age 65.
- The employee has not satisfied the waiting period under the plan. However, the waiting period may not exceed 6 months.
- The employee has elected not to participate in the plan but only if the employee would not have been required to contribute to the cost of other benefits besides group term life insurance if he or she had participated.
- The employee has not satisfied the evidence of insurability required under the plan. However, this evidence of insurability must be determined solely on the basis of a medical questionnaire completed by the employee and not by a medical examination.

The amount of coverage must be a flat amount, a uniform percentage of salary, or an amount based on different employee classifications. These employee classifications, which are referred to as coverage brackets in Sec. 79, may be determined in the manner described earlier. The amount of coverage provided each employee in any classification may be no greater than 2 1/2 times the amount of coverage provided each employee in the next lower classification. In addition, each employee in the lowest classification must be provided with an amount of coverage that is equal to at least 10 percent of the amount provided each employee in the highest classification. There must also be a reasonable expectation that there will be at least one employee in each classification. The following benefit schedule would be unacceptable for two reasons. First, the amount of coverage provided for the hourly employees is only 5 percent of the amount of coverage provided for the president. Second, the amount of coverage on the supervisor is more than 2 1/2 times the amount of coverage provided for the hourly employees.

Classification	Amount of Coverage
President	$100,000
Supervisor	40,000
Hourly employees	5,000

The following benefit schedule, however, would be acceptable:

Classification	Amount of Coverage
President	$100,000
Supervisor	40,000
Hourly employees	20,000

If a group insurance plan that covers fewer than 10 employees does not qualify for favorable tax treatment under Sec. 79, any premiums paid by the employer for such coverage will represent taxable income to the employees. The employer, however, will still receive an income tax deduction for any premiums paid on behalf of the employees, as long as overall compensation is reasonable.

Income Taxation of Proceeds

In most instances the death proceeds under a group term insurance contract do not result in any taxable income to the beneficiary if they are paid in a lump sum. If the proceeds are payable in installments over more than one taxable year of the beneficiary, only the interest earnings attributable to the proceeds will be included in the beneficiary's income for tax purposes. The IRS has issued proposed regulations to clarify the taxation of accelerated benefits, including accelerated benefits from a group policy. The regulations are subject to revision as a result of public comments, but it appears that accelerated benefits will be income tax-free if made as the result of a terminal illness that is expected to result in death within 12 months of payment.

Prior to the Tax Reform Act of 1986, a spouse could exclude the first $1,000 of interest from gross income if it was paid under any settlement option other than an interest-only option. This exclusion is no longer available with respect to proceeds payable as the result of a death occurring after October 22, 1986. Under certain circumstances the exemption of the proceeds from income taxation does not apply if the coverage was transferred (either in whole or in part) for a valuable consideration. Such a situation will arise when the stockholder-employees of a corporation name each other as beneficiaries under their group term insurance coverage as a method of funding a buy-sell agreement. The mutual agreement to name each other as beneficiaries is the valuable consideration. Under these circumstances any proceeds paid to a beneficiary constitute ordinary income to the extent that the proceeds exceed the beneficiary's tax basis, as determined by the Internal Revenue Code.

In many cases benefits paid by an employer to employees or their beneficiaries from the firm's assets receive the same tax treatment as benefits provided under an insurance contract. This is not true for death benefits. If they are provided other than through an insurance contract, the amount of the proceeds in excess of $5,000 will represent taxable income to the beneficiary. For this reason employers are less likely to use alternative funding arrangements for death benefits than for disability and medical expense benefits.

Treatment of Added Coverages

Supplemental life insurance can be written as either a separate contract or as part of the contract providing basic group term life insurance coverage. If it is a separate contract and if the supplemental group life insurance meets the conditions of qualifying as group term insurance under Sec. 79, the amount of coverage provided is added to all other group term insurance for purposes of calculating the Uniform Premium Table I cost. Any premiums paid by the employee for the supplemental coverage reduce the taxable income resulting from the coverage. In all other ways, supplemental life insurance is treated the same as group term insurance.

When supplemental life insurance coverage is written in conjunction with a basic group life insurance plan, employers have the option of treating the supplemental coverage as a separate policy of insurance as long as the premiums are properly allocated between the two portions of the coverage. There is no advantage in treating the supplemental coverage as a separate policy if it, by itself, would still qualify as group term insurance under Sec. 79. However, this election will minimize taxable income to employees if the cost of the supplemental coverage is paid entirely by the employees and all employees are charged rates that are at or below Table I rates. There is no taxable income if the employee pays the entire cost of the coverage.

Premiums paid for accidental death and dismemberment insurance are considered to be health insurance premiums rather than group term insurance premiums. However, these are also deductible to the employer as an ordinary and necessary business expense the same as they are for group term insurance. Benefits paid to an employee under the dismemberment portion of the coverage are treated like benefits received under a health insurance contract and are received income tax free. Death benefits received under the coverage are treated like death benefits received under group term life insurance.

For federal tax purposes, survivor income benefit insurance is considered to be a group term insurance coverage. Under Sec. 79, the amount of benefit is equal to the commuted value of benefit payments that would have been received by eligible survivors if the employee had died during the year. This amount normally is provided annually by the insurance company. A commuted value is also used for estate tax purposes. In all other respects survivor income benefit insurance is treated the same as group term insurance.

Employer contributions for dependent life insurance coverage are fully deductible by the employer as an ordinary and necessary business expense if overall compensation of the employee is reasonable. Employer contributions do not result in taxable income to an employee as long as the value of the benefit is *de minimis*. This means that the value is so small that it is administratively impractical for the employer to account for the cost on a per-person basis. Dependent coverage of $2,000 or less on any person falls into this category. The Internal Revenue Service considers amounts of coverage in excess of $2,000 on any dependent to be more than *de minimis*. If more than $2,000 of coverage is provided for any dependent from employer contributions, the cost of the entire amount of coverage for that dependent (as determined by Uniform Premium Table I rates) will be considered taxable income to the employee.

Death benefits will be free of income taxation and will not be included in the taxable estate of the dependent for estate tax purposes.

State Taxation

In most instances state tax laws affecting group term insurance are similar to the federal laws. However, two major differences do exist. In most states the payment of group term insurance premiums by the employer will not result in any taxable income to the employee, even if the amount of insurance exceeds $50,000. In addition, death proceeds receive favorable tax treatment under the estate and inheritance tax laws of most states. Generally the death proceeds are partially, if not totally, exempt from such taxation.

GROUP LIFE INSURANCE WITH PERMANENT BENEFITS

With the exception of the income tax liability of employees, group paid-up insurance and group ordinary insurance are treated in essentially the same manner as group term insurance. Favorable tax treatment for the term portion of group insurance contracts that have permanent benefits (that is, cash value life insurance) has been available for many years to employees under Sec. 79, if certain requirements are satisfied. However, no favorable tax treatment is given to the premium for the permanent portion of the coverage. If paid by an employer, the premiums for permanent coverage will be fully taxable to the employee as additional compensation.

The Sec. 79 regulation pertaining to group insurance with permanent benefits can be divided into three segments:

- the general requirements that a policy having permanent benefits must satisfy in order to have a portion of the policy considered as group term life insurance for purposes of Sec. 79

- a mandatory actuarial procedure for determining the cost of the permanent benefits
- the provisions for the tax treatment of dividends

General Requirements

The regulations define a *policy* as including two or more obligations of an insurer (for its affiliates) that are offered to a group of employees as a result of their employment relationship. The definition is broad enough to include a group of individual policies provided to a group of employees. In addition, term insurance benefits and permanent benefits provided under separate contracts can be considered a policy, even if one of the benefits is provided to employees who decline the other. The regulations also specify that a *permanent benefit* is an economic value extending beyond one policy year. This includes, for example, paid-up insurance or cash surrender values.

Before any part of a policy may be treated as group term life insurance, two requirements must be met:[1]

- The policy or the employer must designate in writing the portion of each employee's death benefit that is considered group term insurance.
- The portion of each employee's death benefit that is designated as group term insurance for any policy year must not be less than the difference between the total death benefit provided under the policy and the employee's *deemed death benefit*[2] at the end of the policy year.

If these requirements are met, the portion of the policy representing group term insurance will receive favorable income tax treatment under Sec. 79. When added to any other coverage that qualifies for Sec. 79 treatment, only the cost of the total term protection that exceeds $50,000 will represent taxable income to an employee. The cost is calculated by using Uniform Premium Table I rates and is reduced by the aggregate of any employee contributions for the entire term coverage but not for the permanent coverage.

The Cost of Permanent Benefits

The regulations also establish a mandatory allocation procedure of determining the cost of permanent benefits for an employee in a given policy year.[3] This cost represents taxable income to the employee to the extent that it is paid by the employer. It should be noted that the cost as determined by this formula is independent of the annual premium for permanent benefits actually specified in the policy. For example, if an employee is required to pay the cost of permanent benefits and this cost is specified in the policy as $300, the employee will have taxable income to the extent the mandatory allocation procedure yields a cost in excess of $300.

Treatment of Dividends

If the employer pays the entire cost of the permanent benefits, any dividends that are actually or constructively received by the employee must be included in the employee's income for federal income tax purposes. In all other cases, the amount of dividends included in an employee's taxable income is determined by a formula specified in the regulations.[4] The effect of this formula is that any dividend will result in currently taxable income unless an employee has paid more than the aggregate costs (from the inception of coverage) for the permanent protection, as determined by the mandatory allocation formula.

NOTES

1. In addition, plans covering fewer than 10 lives and providing permanent protection must also satisfy the same requirement described in chapter 3 of *Group Benefits: Basic Concepts and Alternatives* for group term life insurance plans covering fewer than 10 lives.
2. The deemed death benefit for a given policy year is defined as R/Y where
   R = the net level premium reserve at the end of that policy year for all benefits provided to the employee by the policy or, if greater, the cash value of the policy at the end of that policy year
   Y = the net single premium for insurance (the premium for one dollar of paid-up whole life insurance) at the employee's age at the end of that policy year
   R and Y are based on the 1958 CSO Mortality Table and a 4 percent interest rate.
3. The cost of permanent benefits for any employee is $X (DDB^2 - DDB^1)$ where
   DDB^2 = the employee's deemed death benefit at the end of the policy year
   DDB^1 = the employee's deemed death benefit at the end of the preceding policy year
   X = the net single premium for insurance (the premium for one dollar of paid-up whole life insurance) at the employee's attained age at the beginning of the policy year
   X is based on the 1958 CSO Mortality Table and a 4 percent rate.
4. The amount included in an employee's income is $(D + C) - (PI + DI + AP)$ where
   D = the total amount of dividends actually or constructively received under the policy by the employee in the current and all preceding tax years of the employee
   C = the total cost of the permanent benefits for the current and all preceding tax years of the employee (determined under the formulas above)
   PI = the total amount of premium included in the employee's income under the formulas for the current and all preceding tax years of the employee
   DI = the total amount of dividends included in the employee's income under this dividend formula in all preceding tax years of the employee
   AP = the total amount paid for permanent benefits by the employee in the current and all preceding taxable years of the employee

5

Federal Taxation of Group Medical Expense Benefits*

Burton T. Beam, Jr.

In many respects the federal tax treatment of group medical expense premiums and benefits parallels that of other group coverages if they are provided through an insurance company, a Blue Cross-Blue Shield plan, a health maintenance organization, or a preferred-provider organization. Contributions by the employer for an employee's coverage are tax deductible to the employer as long as the overall compensation of the employee is reasonable. Employer contributions are not included in the gross income of the employee. In addition, benefits are not taxable to an employee except when they exceed any medical expenses incurred.

One major difference between group medical expense coverage and other forms of group insurance is that a portion of an employee's contribution for coverage may be tax deductible as a medical expense if that individual itemizes income tax deductions. Under the Internal Revenue Code individuals are allowed to deduct certain medical care expenses (including dental expenses) for which no reimbursement was received. This deduction is limited to expenses (including amounts paid for insurance) that exceed 7.5 percent of the taxpayer's adjusted gross income.

The tax situation may be different if an employer provides medical expense benefits through a self-funded plan (referred to in Section 105 of the Internal Revenue Code as a self-insured medical reimbursement plan), under which employers either (1) pay the providers of medical care directly or (2) reimburse employees for their medical expenses. If a self-funded plan meets certain nondiscrimination requirements for highly compensated employees, the employer can deduct benefit payments as they are made, and the employee will have no taxable income. If a plan is discriminatory, the employer will still receive an income tax deduction. However, all or a portion of the benefits received by "highly compensated individuals," but not by other employees, will be treated as taxable income. A highly compensated individual is (1) one of the five highest-paid officers of the firm, (2) a shareholder who owns more than 10 percent of the firm's stock, or (3) one of the highest-paid 25 percent of all the firm's employees.

*Excerpted from *Group Benefits: Basic Concepts and Alternatives*, 6th ed., by Burton T. Beam, Jr. (Bryn Mawr, Pa.: The American College, 1995).

There are no nondiscrimination rules if a plan is not self-funded and provides benefits through an insurance contract, a Blue Cross-Blue Shield plan, an HMO, or a PPO.

To be considered nondiscriminatory, a self-funded plan must meet certain requirements regarding eligibility and benefits. The plan must provide benefits for 70 percent or more of "all employees," or for 80 percent or more of all eligible employees if 70 percent or more of all employees are eligible. Certain employees can be excluded from the all-employees category without affecting the plan's nondiscriminatory status. These include

- employees who have not completed 3 years of service
- employees who have not attained age 25
- part-time employees. Anyone who works less than 25 hours per week is automatically considered a part-time employee. Persons who work 25 or more hours, but less than 35 hours per week, may also be counted as part-time as long as other employees in similar work for the employer have substantially more hours.
- seasonal employees. Anyone who works less than 7 months of the year is automatically considered a seasonal employee. Persons who work between 7 and 9 months of the year may also be considered seasonal as long as other employees have substantially more months of employment.
- employees who are covered by a collective-bargaining agreement if accident-and-health benefits were a subject of collective bargaining

Even if the plan fails to meet the percentage requirements regarding eligibility, it can still qualify as nondiscriminatory as long as the IRS is satisfied that the plan benefits a classification of employees in a manner that does not discriminate in favor of highly compensated individuals. This determination is made on a case-by-case basis.

To satisfy the nondiscrimination requirements for benefits, the same type and amount of benefits must be provided for all employees covered under the plan regardless of their compensation. In addition, the dependents of other employees cannot be treated less favorably than the dependents of highly compensated individuals. However, because diagnostic procedures are not considered part of a self-funded plan for purposes of the nondiscrimination rule, a higher level of this type of benefit is permissible for highly compensated employees.

If a plan is discriminatory in either benefits or eligibility, highly compensated individuals must include the amount of any "excess reimbursement" in their gross income for income tax purposes. If highly compensated individuals receive any benefits that are not available to all employees covered under the plan, then these benefits are considered an excess reimbursement. For example, if a plan pays 80 percent of covered expenses for employees in general, but 100 percent for highly compensated individuals, the extra 20 percent of benefits constitutes taxable income.

If a self-funded plan discriminates in the way it determines eligibility, then highly compensated individuals will have excess reimbursements for any amounts they receive. The amount of this excess reimbursement is determined by a percentage that is calculated by dividing the total amount of benefits received by highly compensated individuals (exclusive of any other excess reimbursements) by the total amount of benefits paid to all employees (exclusive of any other excess reimbursements).

A plan might discriminate with respect to both eligibility and benefits. Using the previous example, assume a highly compensated individual receives $2,000 in benefits during a certain year. If other employees would only receive 80 percent of this amount (or $1,600), then the highly compensated individual would have received an excess reimbursement of $400. If the plan also discriminates in the area of eligibility, the highly compensated individual will incur additional excess reimbursement. For example, if 60 percent of the benefits (ignoring any benefits already considered excess reimbursement) were given to highly compensated individuals, then 60 percent of the remaining $1,600 ($2,000 − $400), or $960, would be added to the $400, for a total excess reimbursement of $1,360.

If a plan provides benefits only for highly compensated individuals, then all benefits received will be considered an excess reimbursement, as the percentage of total benefits received by the highly compensated group would be 100 percent.

6

Deductions for Entertainment Expenses

Alban Salaman[*]

Entertainment of clients, customers, employees, and associates is an expense that practically every business person incurs. However, such expenses may be disallowed as deductible business expenses unless the strict requirements in the Internal Revenue Code are followed. This reading is intended to highlight the requirements that must be met to obtain the proper deduction for entertainment expenses.

Entertainment Defined

Entertainment is defined in the Treasury regulations as any activity that is considered "entertainment, amusement, or recreation." This includes entertaining at nightclubs, cocktail lounges, theaters, country clubs, or sporting events. It also includes activities satisfying the personal, living, or family needs of a business customer, such as providing food and beverages, a hotel room, or an automobile.[1] No deduction will be allowed for any entertainment or recreation that is lavish or extravagant.[2]

Requirements for Deduction

For an entertainment expense to be deductible, it must first be an "ordinary and necessary" business expense of the taxpayer.[3] *Ordinary* refers to what is customary or usual in that trade or business. In a notable case, a secretary of a bankrupt corporation, upon starting a similar business of his own, paid the debts of the bankrupt corporation in an effort to "reestablish" relations with prior customers. He deducted these amounts paid as ordinary and necessary business expenses. The U.S. Supreme Court denied this deduction on the ground that taxpayers do not ordinarily pay the business obligations of others.[4] When a corporation paid the cost of the wedding reception for the majority stockholder's daughter, the expense was declared not ordinary even though most of the guests

---

[*]Alban Salaman, JD, LLM, CLU, is a partner at Holland and Knight, Washington, D.C. This reading has been revised by James F. Ivers III to reflect current law.

were business customers. Such an expense is not a customary business expenditure.[5]

Necessary is defined as what is appropriate and helpful to the development and maintenance of the taxpayer's business. Generally any expense that is ordinary will also be necessary.

There are additional requirements that apply specifically to entertainment expenses. Unless an entertainment activity is "directly related to" or "associated with" the active conduct of the trade or business,[6] a deduction will be disallowed. Furthermore, the taxpayer must be able to substantiate the entertainment expenditures with adequate records of the business-related event or with other sufficient corroborating evidence.

Directly Related Requirement

The *directly related* requirement generally refers to entertainment provided during a period in which the taxpayer is actively engaged in a business negotiation or discussion.[7] Thus food and beverages served to sales prospects during a business discussion are deductible subject to limitations. Under this requirement the taxpayer must have more than a general expectation of deriving some business benefit at some future, indefinite time. The expenditure must relate to the person with whom the taxpayer engaged in the active conduct of business. Thus the entertainment expenses paid for nonbusiness persons, such as spouses, are excluded here but may qualify under the *associated with* test discussed below.

The primary purpose of any combined business and entertainment activity must not be a social one, but one to further the taxpayer's business. For example, if incidental business discussions take place on hunting or fishing trips, it cannot be said that the principal aspect of the combined business and entertainment was the transaction of business.

The directly related test is also met when the expenditures are made in a clear business setting, such that the recipient knows that the taxpayer has no significant motive other than to further business (for example, the sponsorship of a *hospitality room* at a convention, or the entertainment of business representatives at the opening of a new hotel or theatrical production.)[8] Large parties thrown by the taxpayer, such as a wedding where other than business associates are present, are not deductible under the directly related test as there is no clear business setting, nor is the event related.

The expenses of entertainment are not directly related where there is little or no possibility of engaging in the active conduct of business, such as where the taxpayer is not present or when the distractions are substantial.[9] Discussions at nightclubs, cocktail parties, theaters, or sporting events are generally not considered directly related because of the substantial distractions.

Entertainment for goodwill purposes without business discussions is not deductible under the directly related requirement but may qualify under the *associated with* test discussed below.

Associated-with Requirements

As previously stated, entertainment expenses to promote goodwill (for example, expenses incurred in an effort to obtain new business or to encourage the continuation of existing business relationships) are not deductible under the *directly related* requirements. However, such goodwill entertainment expenses are considered *associated with* the conduct of business and may be deductible if the expenses "directly precede or follow" a bona fide business discussion.[10]

For example, Alan, a manufacturing representative, has complex business discussions during the day with Barbara. At night Barbara is Alan's guest at the theater. His entertainment expenses are deductible, because they are associated with the business as goodwill expenses and directly followed bona fide business discussions. However, if Alan merely invited Barbara, a long-time business associate, to the theater, Alan could not deduct expenses if there was no business discussion before or after the show. Similarly, cocktail parties for business associates and their spouses are not deductible under this test if there were no substantial business discussions preceding or following the party.

"Directly preceding or following" has been interpreted in the regulations to mean that the entertainment occurs on the same day as the business discussions. However, entertainment expenses incurred on a day other than the day of business discussion may still qualify depending on the facts and circumstances. To continue the previous example, assume Barbara lives in Los Angeles and travels to New York for the negotiations. If Barbara takes Alan to the theater the night before the negotiations, such entertainment expenses are still deductible.[11]

Unlike the directly related test, expenses allocable to the entertainment of spouses who are not business associates may be deductible under the associated-with test. Thus if Alan invites Barbara and her spouse to the theater after business negotiations, the entire cost of the spouse's ticket is deductible. If Alan's spouse comes also, the cost of this ticket is also deductible.[12] Stricter rules apply to travel expenses paid for spouses.

Exceptions to the General Requirements

Exceptions to the directly related and associated-with requirements in the Code basically relate to employers' entertainment expenses for their employees. Food and beverages furnished on the business premises to employees, whether for recreational or social purposes (such as Christmas parties or summer picnics), and expenses incurred for business meetings of employees (and stockholders, agents, or directors) are deductible without regard to the directly related or associated-with tests. An employer may also deduct entertainment expenses regarded as compensation to the employee, such as a paid vacation trip.[13]

Although the exceptions to the general rules need not meet directly related or associated-with tests, they still must meet the substantiation requirement discussed below in order to be deductible.

The 50 Percent Limitation

Deductions for all business meal and business entertainment expenses are limited to 50 percent of the amount that is deductible after taking into account all other limitations and restrictions. This rule applies to both business entertainment meals and meals taken while the taxpayer is traveling on business. It does not, however, apply to business travel expenses other than meal expenses.

There are some minor exceptions to the 50 percent rule, including meals provided at meetings of business leagues and meals provided to employees on the employer's business premises. Items that are treated as de minimis fringe benefits are excluded from the limitation. Also if a meal is treated as compensation to the recipient for tax purposes, rather than as entertainment, the limitation does not apply.

The 50 percent limitation increases the aftertax cost of business meals and entertainment. For example, suppose Jane entertains a business client just after a meeting in New York. The total cost of the entertainment is $500. Her deduction is limited to 50 percent. Therefore the deductible amount is $250. If Jane is in a 36 percent bracket, her aftertax cost of the entertainment has been increased by $90 because of the 50 percent limitation ($250 nondeductible portion x .36).

Entertainment Facilities and Tickets

Deductions for expenses paid or incurred in connection with the operation and maintenance of an entertainment facility are generally disallowed. No depreciation deductions may be taken even when a facility is primarily used for business entertainment. By eliminating the deductibility of these expenses, Congress has sought to curtail excessive and abusive use of these facilities under the guise of business entertainment.

Facility refers to any real or personal property (such as a yacht, hunting lodge, swimming pool, apartment, or hotel suite in a resort area) that is owned, rented, or used by taxpayers for recreational, entertainment, or amusement activities. However, certain facilities, such as automobiles or airplanes, that are not necessarily recreational may not fall within the above limitation. Deductions for these items continue to be allowed for business trips. Generally deductions for depreciation and operating costs of facilities, such as yachts, lodges, and so forth, are a thing of the past. Those deductions otherwise allowable to individuals that are not predicated on a business connection (such as interest expense on mortgage debt, real estate taxes, and casualty losses) are still available to the taxpayer who owns a facility used for business entertaining.

Out-of-pocket expenses for entertaining at a facility, such as food and beverages, fall within the general entertainment rules. However, membership dues and fees for business, social, athletic, sporting, luncheon, and country clubs are no longer deductible, regardless of whether the taxpayer uses the club for business purposes. Professional and civic organizations are not considered clubs for this purpose, so membership fees paid to such organizations are not subject to the entertainment rules. They are deductible if they qualify as ordinary and necessary business expenses.[14]

Although fees and membership dues are nondeductible, out-of-pocket expenses incurred while entertaining at a club may be deductible as business expenses if the general requirements described in this reading are met. Such expenses would, of course, be subject to the 50 percent limitation.

Deductions for tickets to entertainment events that qualify as business expenses are limited to the face value of the tickets. The face value limitation will make the premium paid to a scalper, as well as the premium paid to a legitimate ticket agency, nondeductible. The deduction, of course, is then further reduced by the 50 percent limitation.

Business Gifts

The deduction for business gifts that are ordinary and necessary business expenses will be disallowed to the extent they exceed $25 per donee.[15] A husband and wife are considered one donor, and they are limited to $25 per donee.[16] Gifts to spouses of business associates are deemed to be gifts to the business associate, unless the spouse is also a bona fide business associate of the taxpayer.[17]

Gifts of admission tickets to business associates for such entertainment as the theater or sporting events are considered *entertainment expenses* if the taxpayer accompanies the associates to the event. Thus the taxpayer would have to meet the associated-with test to obtain a deduction. The directly related test could not be met because of the distractions of such places.

On the other hand, if the taxpayer does not accompany the associates to the place of entertainment, the taxpayer has the choice of treating the expense as either a gift ($25 deduction limit) or *entertainment* (meeting the associated-with test) in order for it to be deductible. The taxpayer will probably elect to treat the expense as associated-with business only when the cost of the admission ticket is in excess of $25 and the event either precedes or follows a business discussion.

Substantiation Requirement

Even if the taxpayer meets the previously discussed requirements and limitations, entertainment expense deductions will be disallowed unless the taxpayer can adequately substantiate the deductible expenses.[18] This requires the taxpayer either to maintain an account book or diary in which entertainment expenditures are recorded at or near the time of expenditure, or to substantiate the deductions with other sufficient evidence. The use of an account book is the better way to meet the substantiation requirements, and it must include the following:

- the amount of each expenditure
- the date of the entertainment and its duration
- the place of the entertainment, including name and address
- the business purpose
- the business relationship, meaning the name, title, or other description of the person entertained, sufficient to establish a business relationship to the taxpayer[19]

If the entertainment is merely associated with the taxpayer's business, then the taxpayer must record the place and duration of the business discussion and must identify the persons entertained who participated in the discussion.[20]

If the entertainment expenditure is $75 or more or for lodging while traveling away from home, documentary evidence, such as a receipt, is necessary to support the deduction.[21] Items incidental to entertainment, such as taxi fares or telephone calls, may be aggregated on a daily basis.[22]

The statutory substantiation requirements superseded the well-known *Cohan* case,[23] which held that if evidence indicated the taxpayer had incurred deductible entertainment expenses, but these amounts could not be determined, then a court must make "as close an approximation as it can, rather than disallow the deduction entirely."

The substantiation requirements have been construed to require a detailed accounting.[24] For example, in one case the taxpayer offered a virtual blizzard of more than 1,700 chits, bills, and statements to support his deductions. The court denied the deduction, holding that his bills contained only monthly aggregates of time, place, or individual amount, and that almost all the exhibits failed to contain a record of the business purpose or business relationship of the persons entertained.[25]

Reporting of Deductible Entertainment Expenses

Depending upon the status of the taxpayer, entertainment expenses may or may not be one of the items deducted in order to determine adjusted gross income. A taxpayer may have more than one status if he or she has more than one business.

If the taxpayer is a sole proprietor or partner, entertainment expenses are considered deductible from gross income to determine adjusted gross income.[26] These taxpayers may deduct such expenses from gross income.[27]

If a partnership pays for or reimburses the entertainment expenses of its partners, the expenses are part of the partnership's deductions from gross income.[28] The partner's share of the taxable income of the partnership after all deductions is added to the partner's individual gross income.[29] If a partner is not reimbursed for entertainment expenses, the partner is allowed to deduct these expenses from gross income to determine adjusted gross income on an individual return, provided that the partnership agreement specifically requires that the partner pay expenses of the partnership without reimbursement.[30]

On the other hand, all employees who have unreimbursed business entertainment expenses must itemize their personal deductions (such as medical expenses or charitable contribution deductions) to take advantage of these entertainment expense deductions.[31] For employees, these deductions are taken from adjusted gross income to determine taxable income and are subject to the 2 percent floor on miscellaneous itemized deductions.

Employees who adequately account to their employer for reimbursed entertainment expenses are entitled to net the reimbursements and deductions in lieu of the more cumbersome method of including the reimbursements as income and then taking the deductions.[32] If reimbursements exceed the deductible expenses, the employee must include this excess income.

If taxpayers are fully reimbursed for their expenses for which they adequately account to their employers, they will not be required to substantiate the expenses again to the Internal Revenue Service.[33] However, the employer and employee must be unrelated for this rule to apply. Employees will have to substantiate expenses if they deduct amounts in excess of their reimbursements.

NOTES

1. Treas. Reg. Sec. 1.274-2(b)(1)(i).
2. Treas. Reg. Sec. 1.274-1.
3. IRC Sec. 162.
4. *Welch v. Helvering,* 290 U.S. 111 (1933).
5. *Shoe Novelty v. Comm'r,* 15 T.C. 517 (1950).
6. IRC Sec. 274(a).
7. Treas. Reg. Sec. 1.274-2(c)(2).

8. Treas. Reg. Sec. 1.274-2(c)(4).

9. Treas. Reg. Sec. 1.274-2(c)(7).

10. S. Rep. no. 1881, 87th Cong. 2d Sess. 26 (1962).

11. Treas. Reg. Sec. 1.274-2(d)(3)(ii).

12. Treas. Reg. Sec. 1.274-2(d)(4).

13. IRC Sec. 274(e).

14. Treas. Reg. Sec. 1.274-2(e)(3)(ii).

15. IRC Sec. 274(b). The $25 limitation relates to the donor's cost rather than to the value of the property at the time of the gift.

16. Treas. Reg. Sec. 1.274-3(e)(2).

17. Treas. Reg. Sec. 1.274-3(d). Under IRC Sec. 274(b)(1)(A) and (B) the following items are not regarded as constituting business gifts but would, of course, be otherwise deductible if incurred in connection with a taxpayer's trade or business: an item costing $4 or less on which the taxpayer's name is clearly and permanently imprinted, and which is one of a number of identical items generally distributed, such as pens, desk sets, plastic bags, calendars, and cases; signs, display racks, or other promotional material to be used on the business premises of the donee.

18. IRC Sec. 274(d).

19. IRC Sec. 274(d); Treas. Reg Sec. 1.274-5(b).

20. Treas. Reg. Sec. 1.274-5(b)(4).

21. Treas. Reg. Sec. 1.274-5(c)(2)(iii); IRS Notice 95-50.

22. Treas. Reg. Sec. 1.274-5(c)(6)(i)(b).

23. *Cohan v. Comm'r*, 39 F.2d 540 (2d Cir. 1930).

24. *Phillip Handelman v. Comm'r*, 509 F.2d 1067 (2d Cir. 1975).

25. *Dowell v. U.S.*, 36 AFTR 75 6314 (5th Cir. 1975). Also see *Earle v. Comm'r*, 28 T.C.M. 138 (1969).

26. IRC Sec. 62(a)(2).

27. Sole proprietors report these deductions on Schedule C of the 1040 Form.

28. These expenses are reported by the partnership on IRS Form 1065.

29. The partner must file Form 1065 K-1 with his or her individual return.

30. *Wallendal v. Comm'r*, 31 T.C. 1249 (1962).

31. Employees must report such expenses under miscellaneous deductions on Schedule A of the 1040 Form.

32. Treas. Reg. Sec. 1.274-5(e)(2).

33. Treas. Reg. Sec. 1.274-5(e)(2)(ii).

7

Charitable Contribution Deductions*

Stephan R. Leimberg

People make gifts to charity. Whether motivated by a combination of social, moral, or economic reasons, individuals have traditionally contributed large amounts to public charities. The vastness of both these sums and the possible tax savings to individuals makes it imperative for the financial planner to have a working knowledge of the charitable contribution deduction rules.

Charitable contributions have tax value. They result in a current income tax savings, they may reduce federal estate taxes, and they can be made gift tax free. From the charity's point of view, charitable contributions are also tax favored; the charity itself pays no tax upon the receipt of either a lifetime gift or a bequest, and generally no income tax is paid by the qualified charity on income earned by donated property.

A charitable contribution deduction is allowed for contributions to certain charitable, religious, scientific, educational, and other specified organizations. Deductions may be taken by either individuals or corporations. The deduction by individual taxpayers is allowed only from adjusted gross income; therefore it may be wise from a tax standpoint for individuals to make charitable contributions only in years in which they have itemized deductions in excess of the standard deduction amount.

FOUR REQUIREMENTS FOR DEDUCTIBILITY

The first requirement for deductible charitable contributions is that they must be made to organizations that are *qualified*. Qualified organizations include nonprofit schools and hospitals, churches and synagogues, the United Fund, community chests, YMCA, YMHA, YWCA, YWHA, the American Red Cross, the Salvation Army, and police boys' clubs. The Boy Scouts, Campfire Girls, CARE, the Heart Association, and The American College are some of the other organizations that are considered qualified.[1]

A donee cannot be considered a qualified charity unless it meets three conditions. First, it must be an organization operated exclusively for religious, charitable, scientific, literary, or educational purposes, or for the prevention of cruelty to children or animals. Second, no part of the organization's earnings can

---

*This reading has been updated by James F. Ivers III to reflect current law.

benefit any private shareholder or similar individual. Third, no substantial part of such an organization's work can consist of propaganda or legislation-influencing activities.

Technically there are two types of qualified charities: (1) the public charity and (2) the private charity. Gifts to public charities are subject to higher deductible limits than gifts to private charities. Public charities (also called 50 percent charities because individuals can take a deduction of up to 50 percent of their contribution base for gifts to these charities) include most well-known charities such as the American Red Cross, the United Way, and The American College. All other qualified charities that are not public (50 percent) charities are considered private (20 or 30 percent) charities. (See the Charitable Contribution Deduction Limitations Chart later in this reading.) Included under the category of private charities would be most private foundations or organizations. It is important to recognize that an organization is not automatically a qualified charity merely because it is tax exempt.

For example, civic associations, social clubs, chambers of commerce, and other business leagues are generally exempt from tax. However, they are not considered qualified organizations. Therefore gifts to these organizations are not deductible as charitable contributions, but they may be deductible as ordinary and necessary business expenses. Even direct contributions of cash or other property to a needy family are generally nondeductible because of the rule that contributions must be made to a qualified charity to be deductible.

A second requirement necessary for a charitable contribution deduction is that *property* must be the subject of the gift. The value of a taxpayer's time or services, even if contributed to a qualified charity, is not deductible. For example, if Whipsaw, a carpenter, spent 10 hours building a podium for his church, he could not deduct his normal hourly wage as a charitable contribution. However, if he built the podium at home and gifted it to the church, he could deduct the cost of the materials used in producing the finished product (not including the value of his working time) as a charitable contribution.

If Marlon Brandi — the famous streetcar conductor turned actor — entertained at a charity ball, he could not deduct the value of his personal services, mainly because he has not been charged with income as the result of rendering such services. However, he could deduct any out-of-pocket expenses incurred in rendering such services. For example, if he had to fly into New York from Chicago solely to appear at the charitable event, his transportation expenses incurred in rendering services for the charity in question would be deductible.

A third requirement for a charitable contribution deduction is that there must in fact be a contribution to the charity in excess of the value received. In some cases, donors will receive a benefit in conjunction with their charitable gifts. Such contributions are deductible only to the extent that the value of the contributed property exceeds any consideration or benefit to the donor. For example, if Pam purchases bonds issued by a nonprofit hospital to finance a new building, the purchase price of the bond would not be deductible as a contribution. However, if Pam later donated the bonds to the hospital, she would then become entitled to a deduction. A similar question often arises in the case of dues, fees, or assessments paid to qualified organizations. These items are deductible as contributions only to the extent that they exceed the monetary value of benefits received by the *donor*. Charitable organizations are now required to inform donors of the extent to which the contribution exceeds the value of benefits received in return if the contribution is more than $75. Dues, fees, or assessments paid to country clubs, veterans and fraternal organizations, or lodges are specifically nondeductible as charitable contributions.

If the local church or synagogue was to sponsor a bingo night, amounts paid to play (or for raffle tickets or other games of chance) would not be considered contributions. They would be treated as wagering losses. Likewise, if a qualified charitable organization sponsors a picnic (or a night at the theater, a charity ball, a sporting event, or a show), only the difference between the fair market value of the picnic lunch purchased and the amount actually paid is considered a charitable contribution. The balance is treated as a nondeductible personal expenditure. For example, if you paid $20 for a box lunch at a church picnic and the lunch plus entertainment was worth $3, only the difference—$17—would be a charitable contribution assuming the entire net proceeds of the picnic went to the church. The $3 balance is considered a personal outlay that is specifically nondeductible.

It is often difficult to distinguish between a tax-deductible *contribution to charity* and a nondeductible personal expense. A commonly litigated example is the cost of tuition paid by taxpayers to a parochial school for their children. Even where the tuition payment was not legally required by the church (only *expected*), no deduction was allowed because the outlay was considered essentially an expense in payment of personal educational services received rather than a charitable contribution.

A fourth requirement that must be met for a deduction to be allowed is that the contribution must actually be paid in cash or other property before the close of the tax year in question. This rule applies regardless of the accounting method used by the taxpayer. In other words, even an accrual-basis taxpayer must actually pay cash or contribute other property before the close of the tax year. A contribution made by credit charge is equivalent to payment in cash when the charge is made. Taxpayers are entitled to charitable deductions in the year they charge the contributions to their bank credit cards and not in the year they actually make payment to the bank.

Often a donor will give a charitable organization a promissory note. The issuance and even the delivery of the note are not enough to meet the requirement that the contribution be paid within the tax year. However, the donor will be allowed a deduction when payments on the note are actually made.

Deductible contributions of $250 or more are now subject to substantiation requirements involving a written acknowledgment from the donee organization that must be either provided to the donor or reported in substance to the IRS.

DEDUCTIBLE AMOUNTS

Taxpayers are entitled to a deduction for contributions to qualified charities; that is, governmental bodies, public or private corporations, trusts, and foundations organized as well as operated predominantly for charitable, religious, scientific, literary, or educational purposes. However, the taxpayer's deduction is limited.

The amount of a charitable contribution deduction depends on the following five factors, which will be discussed in detail:

1. *the type of property given away.* This reading will consider the following items under the heading of *property:* (a) rent-free occupancy, (b) cash, (c) capital-gain property, (d) ordinary-income property, (e) tangible personal property where the use of that property by the donee is related to the exempt functions of the donee, (f) tangible personal property where the use of that property is unrelated to the exempt purposes of the donee, and (g) future interests in property.

2. *the identity of the donee.* Generally contributions to publicly supported domestic organizations—so-called "public charities"—are more favorably treated than contributions to foreign organizations or most private foundations. The deduction for an individual's contributions to nonpublic (private) charities, regardless of the type of property given away, is limited to the lesser of (a) 20 or 30 percent (see chart) of the taxpayer's contribution base, which is basically adjusted gross income (AGI), or (b) 50 percent of the taxpayer's contribution base, minus the amount of charitable contribution deductions allowed for contributions to the public-type charities. For example, if Richblood donates property worth 40 percent of his contribution base (AGI) to a public charity, such as the Boy Scouts, his additional contributions to 20 or 30 percent charities (private charities) are deductible only up to 10 percent of his contribution base. Donations to individuals are not deductible.

3. *the identity of the contributor.* Individuals are limited to specified percentages of adjusted gross income, while a corporation is limited to a deduction based on a percentage of its taxable income.

4. *the amount of property given away.* Generally there is a carryover of excess contributions—contributions above their deductible limit—for up to 5 years. (See the Charitable Contribution Deduction Limitations Chart on the following page.)

CHARITABLE CONTRIBUTION DEDUCTION LIMITATIONS CHART

Type of Property	Donee	Percentage Limitation		Excess Carryover*		Amount Deductible
		Individual Adjusted Gross Income	Corporation Taxable Income	Individual	Corporation	
(1)	(2)	(3)	(4)	(5)	(6)	(7)
(A) Rent-free occupancy	Public					No deduction
	Private					No deduction
(B) Cash	Public	50%	10%	5 yrs.	5 yrs.	Full deduction
	Private	30%	10%	5 yrs.	5 yrs.	Full deduction
(C) Capital-gain property (1) Real estate and intangible personal property	Public	30% or	10%	5 yrs.	5 yrs.	Full deduction for fair market value (FMV)
		50% on election (see column 7)	No corp. election	5 yrs.		FMV less 100% of appreciation (donor's cost basis)†
	Private	20%	10%	5 yrs.	5 yrs.	Donor's cost basis
(2) Tangible personal property Use related	Public	30% or	10%	5 yrs.	5 yrs.	Full deduction for FMV
		50% on election		5 yrs.		Donor's cost basis
Use unrelated	Private	20%	10%	5 yrs.	5 yrs.	Donor's cost basis
	Public	50%	10%	5 yrs.	5 yrs.	Donor's cost basis
	Private	20%	10%	5 yrs.	5 yrs.	Donor's cost basis
(D) Ordinary-income property	Public	50%	10%	5 yrs.	5 yrs.	Donor's cost basis
	Private	30%	10%	5 yrs.	5 yrs.	Donor's cost basis

* No carryback
† Example: Basis - $3,000. FMV - $5,000. 100% of appreciation = $2,000. Therefore deduction limited to $3,000 ($5,000 − $2,000).

5. *the place where the charity is organized.* Gifts made to foreign charities are not deductible (except where allowed by treaty).

As mentioned above, the actual amount of charitable contribution deduction depends on a number of factors. The primary questions to ask in each case are the following: (a) What type of property was gifted? (b) Was the donee a private organization or publicly supported? (c) Was the donor an individual or a corporation? (d) How much property was given? In order to illustrate the effect of these factors on the amount of charitable contribution deduction that will be allowed in a given case, review the chart on page 57 as well as the accompanying text.

DEDUCTIBLE CONTRIBUTIONS

Right to Use Property

Contributions consisting of a mere right to use property (such as a rent-free lease to the Boy Scouts) are not deductible. To be deductible, contributions must be made in cash or other property. The mere right to use property is considered neither cash nor other property. The IRS considers a contribution of the right to use property as a contribution of less than the donor's entire interest in the property.

Generally a charitable contribution of less than a donor's entire interest in property is nondeductible. Gifts of a partial interest in property are deductible in the following three narrowly defined situations:

1. The first is a gift of an undivided portion of the donor's entire interest. For example, if Xavier gave his original Ramlo sculpture to the Philadelphia Museum of Art but agreed with the museum that he could keep it as long as he or his wife lived, no current deduction would be allowed. However, if Xavier gave an undivided one-half interest in the sculpture (that is, if he gave the museum an immediate, absolute, and complete right of ownership for display purposes or otherwise) for one-half of each year, he would likely be successful in obtaining a current deduction.
2. The second situation involves a gift of a remainder interest in a personal residence or farm. If Tammy gives a qualified organization her home or farm with the stipulation that she may live there for life, Tammy may take a current income tax deduction for the present value of the future gift. This assumes, of course, that the gift is irrevocable.
3. Finally, a gift of a partial interest would be deductible if transferred in trust. This exception allows a charitable deduction for outright transfers

of property, even if less than the taxpayer's entire interest is transferred. The deduction is allowed to the same extent that a deduction would be allowed had the same property been transferred in trust rather than directly to the charitable organization. Gifts in trust will be discussed in detail later in this reading.

Cash

Depending upon who is the donee, cash contributions are fully deductible subject to a maximum that is a percentage of adjusted gross income. If the donee is a publicly supported charity, the deduction ceiling is 50 percent of the individual taxpayer's adjusted gross income. The deduction ceiling for private charities is 30 percent of adjusted gross income. A corporation's deduction is limited to 10 percent of its taxable income (with certain adjustments). Regardless of the type of property gifted, a corporation can always take a current deduction of 10 percent of its taxable income (column 4 of the Charitable Contribution Deduction Limitations Chart). Likewise, regardless of the identity of the donee, a corporation may carry over excess contributions for up to 5 years (column 6 of the Charitable Contribution Deduction Limitations Chart).

Individuals who make contributions to public organizations in excess of the deductible limit for the taxable year may carry over their excess deductions (columns 5 and 6 of the Charitable Contribution Deduction Limitations Chart) for a period of up to 5 years. In other words, excess contributions are not wasted and can be used as itemized deductions in future years. For example, if Goldberg contributed $20,000 in cash to a synagogue this year, but his adjusted gross income was only $36,000, he could currently deduct only 50 percent of his adjusted gross income, which is $18,000. However, he could carry over the $2,000 excess ($20,000 contribution minus $18,000) to next year. Individuals who make excess cash contributions to private charities may deduct the excess contributions in subsequent years.

A full deduction, up to the percentage limitation of 50 percent of adjusted gross income for individuals (or 10 percent of taxable income for corporations), is allowed for gifts of cash to a public charity (column 7 of the Charitable Contribution Deduction Limitations Chart).

If a taxpayer makes a contribution to a college or university and receives the right to purchase tickets for an athletic event in one of the institution's athletic stadiums as a result of the contribution, only 80 percent of the amount contributed will be deductible by the taxpayer. This provision applies to contributions made, for example, by an alumnus of a university that requires the alumnus to make the contribution in order to be eligible to purchase season tickets for the university's basketball team.

Capital-Gain Property

Capital-gain property is property that would have produced a long-term capital gain on the date of the gift had it been sold rather than donated to charity. Capital-gain property can be divided into two types. The first type would consist of intangible personal property and all real property. A gift of Xerox stock purchased 11 years ago at $100 a share, now worth $400 a share, would be considered intangible, personal, capital-gain property. Appreciated land that is held the requisite holding period would be an example of real property properly classified as capital-gain property. The second type of capital-gain property is tangible personal property, such as a car, a painting, a sculpture, an antique, or jewelry. Tangible personal property will be discussed later in this reading.

Where intangible personal property or real property is given to a public donee (column 2 of the Charitable Contribution Deduction Limitations Chart), an individual's deduction may not exceed 30 percent of adjusted gross income (column 3 of the Charitable Contribution Deduction Limitations Chart). If the gift exceeds this percentage limitation, the taxpayer may carry over the deduction for up to 5 future years (column 5 of the Charitable Contribution Deduction Limitations Chart). The full fair market value of the gift is deductible (column 7 of the Charitable Contribution Deduction Limitations Chart).

For example, suppose Phil Anthropist donates stock worth $25,000 to the Gotham Library. The stock cost Phil $13,000 when he purchased it 4 years ago. If Phil's adjusted gross income was $30,000, his maximum contribution deduction would be $9,000 (30 percent of $30,000). He would be able to carry over the $16,000 balance and apply that as a deduction against future years' income.

There is an election that taxpayers may want to make in situations similar to the example above. The 30 percent limit can be increased to 50 percent of adjusted gross income if donors are willing to reduce the value of their gifts by 100 percent of their potential gain. In other words, Phil, in the example above, could elect to exclude 100 percent of his potential gain, $12,000, thus decreasing the deductible value to $13,000 ($25,000 minus $12,000). By doing so, he is currently able to deduct the entire $13,000. This is because the election allows him to currently deduct up to 50 percent of his adjusted gross income of $30,000.

The election can be important for a taxpayer whose income fluctuates widely from year to year. It is of particular value when the amount of appreciation is small. For example, capital-gain property with a basis of $980 and a fair market value of $1,000 would be reduced by only $20. In this way taxpayers could qualify for the higher 50 percent limitation at the expense of losing only a very small portion of their deductions. However, note that the amount representing 100 percent of the potential gain may not be carried over and deducted in a later year if the election is made. Note that by reducing the deductible amount by 100 percent of the potential gain, the deduction is, in effect, limited to the donor's basis in the property.

Ordinary-Income Property

Ordinary-income property is an asset that would have resulted in ordinary income (rather than capital gain) on the date of contribution had it been sold at its fair market value rather than contributed. Ordinary-income property includes (1) capital assets held 12 months or less at the time contributed; (2) works of art, books, letters, and musical compositions, but only if given by the person who created or prepared them or for whom they were prepared; and (3) a business person's stock in trade and inventory (which would result in ordinary income if sold).

Other than the special exception discussed in the following paragraph, taxpayers' deductions are limited to their basis (cost) for ordinary-income property (column 7 of the Charitable Contribution Deduction Limitations Chart). For example, if Papa Chezman, the famous painter, donated a genuine Chezman painting worth $25,000 to an art museum, his deduction would be limited to his cost for producing the painting. This means that only the cost for canvas, paint, etc., would be deductible. No deduction would be allowed for the value of his time. Here is a similar situation: Phil Anthropist owned his National Motors stock for 5 months. A sale would have resulted in short-term capital gain. He purchased the stock at a cost of $12,000 and gave it to the Boy Scouts of America when it was worth $25,000. Only his cost (basis) is deductible. Therefore, since the property is considered ordinary-income property, Phil will be limited to a charitable deduction of $12,000 even though the property had a fair market value of $25,000 at the time of the gift.

One exception increases the charitable deduction for contributions by corporations of new tangible inventory-type property that is used for scientific research. As an increased incentive to corporations to make charitable contributions of scientific equipment to colleges or universities, a deduction is allowed in an amount equal to the cost of the property plus one-half of the unrealized appreciation limited to a maximum deduction of twice the basis of the property. In other words, the charitable deduction in such cases cannot exceed twice the cost of the property regardless of the amount of the unrealized appreciation. The property that qualifies for this increased deduction must be either new inventory-type scientific equipment or an apparatus manufactured by the donor corporation. This rule applies only to contributions of scientific equipment to colleges, universities, and certain research organizations to be used for research purposes, including research training. The property must be donated to a college or university no later than 2 years after it was fully constructed or purchased. This deduction is available to business corporations only.

S corporations, personal holding companies, and certain service organizations are not eligible for the increased deduction.

Ordinary-income property gifted to a public charity is subject to the 50-percent-of-AGI limitation. Consequently, in the previous example, Phil Anthropist would need an AGI of at last $24,000 to deduct $12,000 for his gift to the Boy Scouts if the property given had been ordinary-income property (rather than long-term capital-gain property).

Gifts of ordinary-income property should be avoided where the estate will be subject to federal estate taxes. Ordinary-income property left by will to charity can be more beneficial, since a federal estate tax deduction for the full value of the property can be taken. However, where it appears that the estate will not be subject to federal estate tax, a lifetime gift of ordinary-income property will permit a current income tax deduction, although it will be somewhat limited, as described previously.

Tangible Personal Property

Tangible personal property (which would have produced capital gain if sold) includes cars, jewelry, sculptures, artworks, books, and so forth, but only if created or produced by persons other than the donor. With respect to this type of property, a distinction must be made between (a) gifts that will be used by the donee-charity in such a manner that the use of the gift is related to the exempt purposes of the donee, and (b) gifts that will not be used by the charity in a manner related to the exempt purposes of the donee.

For example, a gift of a painting (not by the artist) would be *use related* if the painting was donated to a museum that planned to exhibit the painting in its public galleries. The same gift would be *use unrelated* if given to the Red Cross or to the Campfire Girls. It is unlikely that either of these organizations would use the painting as a painting. In all likelihood the art would be sold and the proceeds used for the Red Cross or the Campfire Girls. However, it is the gift itself, and not the cash or other property that can be obtained for the gift, that determines whether the gift is use related or use unrelated.

Another example might be the contribution of a stamp collection to an educational institution. If the stamp collection is placed in the donee-organization's library for display and study by students, the use of the donated property is related to the educational purposes constituting the basis of the charitable organization's tax exemption. But if the stamps are sold, the use of the property is an unrelated one, even if the proceeds are used by the organization for educational purposes.

This distinction is important because where appreciated tangible personal property is considered use related, the entire fair market value at the date of the gift is deductible. In other words, a use-related gift of tangible personal property held for the requisite period is treated exactly the same as any other long-term capital-gain property. Thus the donor is subject to the 30-percent-of-AGI limitation or may elect to reduce the value of the gift by 100 percent of the potential gain realized if the gift was sold rather than contributed. By doing this, the percentage limitation on the donor's adjusted gross income ceiling would be increased to 50 percent. In some cases this would result in a larger, immediate deduction.

For example, Denise Donor has an adjusted gross income of $10,000. She contributes a collection of whaling harpoons for display purposes to the Cape May County Historical Museum (a public charity). The collection cost Denise $6,000, but it was worth $10,000 on the date of contribution. The type of property contributed is tangible personal property. The donee is a public charity, and the gift is use related to the exempt purposes of the museum. Therefore Denise can deduct up to 30 percent of her contribution base (AGI), $10,000, or $3,000. She gets credit for the full $10,000 contribution, enabling her to carry over the excess contribution, $7,000, for up to 5 years (subject to the 30 percent rule each year). Alternatively, Denise may elect to reduce the value of her gift by 100 percent of the potential gain, or $4,000 ($10,000 minus $6,000). Under the election Denise would have a current deduction of $5,000 (50 percent of adjusted gross income), and the remaining $1,000 ($6,000 minus $5,000) could be deducted in a later year.

If the gift is use unrelated (that is, made to a donee whose direct use of the asset is unrelated to the charitable function of the donee), the fair market value of the gift *must* be reduced by 100 percent of the potential gain. For example, the gift by Denise Donor would be *worth* only $6,000. However, it would be deductible up to 50 percent of her contribution base.

Future Interests in Property

A *future interest* is any interest or right that will begin at some time in the future. The term *future interest* includes situations where donors purport to give tangible personal property to a charitable organization but have made a written or oral agreement with the organization reserving to themselves or members of their immediate families the right to use, possess, or enjoy the property. For example, suppose Fulton Flushbucks donates a genuine Meccariello photograph to an art museum but arranges with the museum to keep the photograph in his home for as long as he lives. The museum has only a future interest in the photograph.

Some of the basic rules governing charitable contribution deductions are that contributions must (1) actually be paid, (2) be paid in cash or other property, and (3) be paid before the close of the tax year. Furthermore, no deductions are allowed for a contribution of less than the donor's entire interest in property.

(Three narrow exceptions are the following: (1) an undivided portion of the donor's entire interest, (2) remainder interest in personal residences or farms, or (3) partial interest that would be deductible if transferred in trust.) A charitable contribution (not made by a transfer in trust) of a partial interest in property may not be deducted.

Since the benefit to the museum—and consequently to the public—was deferred in the Flushbucks gift of the Meccariello photograph above, no current tax deduction would be allowed. The implication is that a deduction will not be allowed until the charity receives actual possession or enjoyment of the artwork. The gift of tangible personal property must be complete in the sense that all interests and rights to the possession and enjoyment of the property must vest in the charity. This means that a transfer of a future interest in property to a charity is not deductible until all intervening interests in and rights to possession held by the donor or certain related persons or organizations have expired (or unless the gift is in the form of a future interest in trust that meets the requirements discussed below).

Remainder interests are a form of future interest in which an income interest is given by the donor to someone other than the donor, and at the death of that income beneficiary, the principal goes to a designated charity. An example would be a gift to Sue for life and at the death of Sue (the income beneficiary), the remainder (the principal at the death of Sue) goes to charity (the remainderman). A gift "to Sue for life, remainder to The American College" would be considered a gift of a future interest to The American College. The American College is called the remainderman because the gift *remains* away from the donor after the death of Sue, the income beneficiary, and The American College receives the principal remaining at Sue's death.

GIFTS IN TRUST

Gifts of a remainder interest either in real property or in trust are deductible only if made in one of three ways: (1) a *fixed-annuity* trust, (2) a *unitrust,* or (3) a *pooled-income fund.* These three permissible trust forms are a result of congressional concern over potential abuses of gifts of a remainder interest in trust to charity. For example, suppose Mr. and Mrs. Weltodo were a financially secure but childless couple. Mr. Weltodo might leave his property to his wife in trust. Mrs. Weltodo, according to the terms of the trust, would receive the income for life if she survived her husband. At her death, the principal in the trust would pass to a designated charity. Mr. Weltodo would take a current charitable contribution deduction for the present value of the gift that the charity would receive at the death of the income beneficiary. In order to counteract inflation and provide for contingencies, a clause might be inserted in the trust agreement authorizing an invasion of principal for Mrs. Weltodo's benefit.

The potential for abuse was that the trust principal was often invested in securities that produced an extremely high income but at the cost of a correspondingly high risk. This situation naturally worked to the detriment of the charitable *remainderman.* In addition, the trustee's ability to make substantial invasions into the trust principal further increased the likelihood that little, if any, of the original contribution would be received by the charity. The result was a decrease in the value of the charity's remainder interest.

For these reasons, rules were designed to prevent a taxpayer from receiving a current charitable contribution deduction for a gift to charity of a remainder interest in trust that is substantially in excess of the amount the charity may ultimately receive. (This is so because the assumptions used in calculating the value of the remainder interest had little relation to the actual investment policies of the trust.)

Pursuant to these rules, deductions are basically limited to situations where the trust specifies (1) a fixed annual *amount* that is to be paid to the noncharitable income beneficiary (an annuity trust); or (2) the amount the income beneficiary will receive in terms of a *fixed percentage* of the value of the trust assets ascertained each year (a unitrust); or (3) that property contributed by a number of donors is commingled with property transferred by other donors, and each beneficiary of an income interest will receive income determined by the rate of return earned by the trust for such year (a pooled-income fund).

Annuity Trust

More specifically, a charitable remainder annuity trust is a trust designed to permit payment of a fixed amount annually to a noncharitable (income) beneficiary with the remainder going to charity. In order to qualify for income tax (and estate or gift tax) deductions, the trust must meet a number of tests. The primary requirements are as follows:

- A fixed amount or fixed percentage of the *initial value* of the trust must be payable to the noncharitable beneficiary.
- This annuity must not be less than an amount equal to 5 percent of the initial fair market value of all the property transferred in trust.
- The specified amount must be paid at least annually to the beneficiary out of income and/or principal.
- The trust must be irrevocable and not subject to a power by either the donor, the trustee, or the beneficiary to invade, alter, or amend the trust.
- The trust must be for the benefit of a named individual or individuals who must be living at the time the property is transferred to the trust. An amount can be paid to a person for life or for a term of years, not

greater than 20 years. The remainder must go to charity (charities) and cannot be split between charitable and noncharitable beneficiaries.

If all the necessary tests are met, the donor of a charitable remainder annuity trust will be entitled to an income tax deduction limited to the present value of the remainder interest.

Unitrust

A charitable remainder unitrust, like a charitable remainder annuity trust, is basically designed to permit payment of a periodic sum to a noncharitable beneficiary with a remainder to charity. The key distinction is in how the periodic sum is computed. In order to qualify for income, estate, and gift tax deductions, a charitable remainder unitrust must meet a number of tests, the most important of which are the following:

- A fixed percentage of the net fair market value of the principal, *as revalued annually,* must be payable to the noncharitable beneficiary. Therefore the amount payable to the income beneficiary may fluctuate from year to year.
- The percentage payable must not be less than 5 percent of the annual value.
- The unitrust may provide that the noncharitable beneficiary can receive the lesser of (1) the specified fixed percentage or (2) the trust income for the year, plus any excess trust income to the extent of any deficiency in the prior years by reason of the limitation to the amount of trust income in such years.
- The noncharitable income beneficiaries must be living at the time of transfer in trust, and their interests must be for a term not exceeding 20 years, or for their respective lives.
- The entire remainder must go to charity (or charities).

The tax deductions allowed are the same as in the case of a charitable remainder annuity trust.

Pooled-Income Fund

A pooled-income fund is a trust created and maintained by a public charity rather than a private donor. The basic requirements are the following:

- The donor must contribute an irrevocable, vested remainder interest to the charitable organization that maintains it.

- The property transferred by each donor must be commingled with the property transferred by other donors.
- The fund cannot invest in tax-exempt securities.
- No donor or income beneficiary can be a trustee.
- The donor must retain a life income interest for himself or herself or one or more named income beneficiaries.
- Each income beneficiary must be entitled to and receive a pro rata share of the income (annually) based upon the rate of return earned by the fund.

If these tests are met, the donor will be entitled to income and gift tax deductions. The economic advantage to the donor of making this transfer is that the donor is obtaining diversification for the income beneficiary without incurring the capital-gains tax that would ordinarily be imposed if the donor exchanged securities for other securities.

Advantages of Charitable Gifts of Life Insurance

Life insurance, like any other property, can be and often is the subject of a gift. In fact, life insurance is a favored means of making charitable contributions for a number of reasons.

First, the death benefit going to charity is guaranteed as long as premiums are paid. This means that the charity will receive an amount that is fixed in value and not subject to the potential downside risks of securities.

Second, life insurance provides an *amplified* gift that can be purchased on the installment plan. Through a relatively small annual cost (premium), a large benefit can be provided for the charity. A large gift can be made without impairing or diluting the control of a family business interest or other investments. Assets earmarked for the donor-insured's family can be kept intact.

Third, life insurance is a self-completing gift. If the donor lives, cash values (which can be currently used by the charity) grow constantly from year to year. If the donor becomes disabled, the policy will remain in full force through the waiver-of-premium feature, guaranteeing both the ultimate death benefit to the charity as well as the same cash values and dividend buildup that would have been earned had the insured not become disabled. Even if death occurs after only one deposit, the charity is assured of its full gift.

Fourth, the death proceeds can be received by the designated charity free of federal income and estate taxes, probate and administrative costs and delays, brokerage fees, or other transfer costs. Thus the charity in fact receives one hundred cent dollars. This prompt cash payment should be compared with the payment of a gift to the selected charity under the terms of an individual's will. In that case, probate delays of up to several years are not uncommon.

Fifth, because of the contractual nature of the life insurance contract, large gifts to charity are not subject to attack by disgruntled heirs. Life insurance proceeds also do not violate the so-called mortmain statutes that prohibit or limit gifts made within a short time of death.

Finally, a substantial gift may be made with no attending publicity. Since the life insurance proceeds paid to charity can be arranged so they will not be part of the decedent's probate estate, the proceeds can be paid confidentially. Of course, publicity may be given if desired.

Taxation of Charitable Gifts of Life Insurance

If a life insurance policy was sold at a gain, the gain would be taxed as ordinary income. Therefore a gift of life insurance is a gift of ordinary-income property. Assuming the value of the policy (interpolated terminal reserve plus unearned premium on the date of the sale) exceeds the policyholder's net premium payments, the deduction for a gift of a policy is equal to the policyholder's basis (cost), that is, the net premium payments paid by the policyholder. For example, suppose Mary McClu assigns a policy on her life to The American College. Her charitable contribution deduction is limited to her basis, that is, her cost in the contract (or the value of the policy if lower). If Mary paid net premiums of $15,000, even if the policy had a value of $18,000, her charitable contribution deduction would be limited to $15,000. On the other hand, if the value of the policy in this case was $15,000 and the net premium payments were $18,000, the amount of the charitable deduction would be $15,000. The amount of the deduction for a paid-up policy is dependent on the replacement cost of the policy. The insurance company in question will generally calculate the exact value on IRS Form 712 upon request.

The replacement cost of a single-premium or paid-up policy is the single premium the same insurer would charge for a policy of the same amount at the insured's attained age (increased by the value of any dividend credits, and reduced by the amount of any loans outstanding).

The charitable deduction for a newly issued policy is the gross premium paid by the insured.

Premium Payments as Contributions

Premium payments are considered gifts of cash and therefore are fully and currently deductible as charitable contributions if the charity owns the policy outright.

Occasionally, a donor will attempt to *split dollar* the charitable gift; that is, name the donor's personal beneficiary as the recipient of the policy's pure death benefit (the amount at risk), but make the charity the owner of the cash value.

The IRS has maintained that this is a gift of a "partial interest" in property and denies a deduction for the premium payment. The same principle applies where the donor retains an interest in the policy cash value but assigns an interest in the *amount-at-risk* portion to the charity. Therefore the donor should make an absolute assignment of the ownership of the policy to the charity in order to qualify for the desired tax benefits. If the charity initially applies for and owns a life insurance policy, and the insured pays the premiums, the charity must have an insurable interest in the insured under local law in order for the insured to obtain the desired tax benefits. In general, it may be preferable to transfer ownership of an existing policy.

The donor should send a check directly to the charity and have it pay the premium to the life insurance company in order to ensure the most favorable tax results. The cancelled check will serve as proof (1) of the fact that a gift was made to the charity, (2) of the date the gift was made, and (3) of the amount of the gift. It will also ensure a full deduction of up to 50 percent of the donor's adjusted gross income.

There should be no adverse gift or estate tax implications. Gifts to charity are deductible in full for federal gift tax purposes. There is no percentage limitation on the amount of the gift tax deduction. Likewise, the death proceeds of a life insurance policy payable to a charity do not generate any federal estate tax.

NOTE

1. A list of qualified organizations is contained in IRS publication no. 78, entitled "Cumulative List, Organizations Described in Section 170(c) of the Internal Revenue Code of 1986," published by the Superintendent of Documents, U.S. Government Printing Office in Washington, D.C. A taxpayer is not entitled to rely on the statements of an organization as to whether contributions to it are tax deductible.

8

Income Taxation of Life and Health Insurance[*]

Fred J. Dopheide[†]

Life insurance has received favorable tax treatment since 1916 when the federal income tax law first exempted life insurance death benefits from taxation. Although the laws concerning taxation of life insurance have changed since then, Congress has continued to recognize both the social value and utility of sheltering life insurance from the erosion of the federal income tax.

It is the purpose of this reading to present the general rules of income taxation of life and health insurance as well as to discuss the tax consequences of certain specific life insurance arrangements. In examining these arrangements, the following three interrelated questions are discussed:

1. When are proceeds received at death or as living benefits subject to income taxation?
2. When are premiums a deductible item for income tax purposes?
3. When are premiums paid by an individual or entity taxable to the party receiving the economic benefit from such payment?

GENERAL RULES

Life Insurance Death Benefits

Lump-Sum Payments

Generally, life insurance death benefits payable by reason of death of the insured are excluded from the gross income of the beneficiary,[1] regardless of whether the beneficiary is an individual or an entity. In addition to death benefits payable under individual life insurance policies, the term *death benefit payments,*

---

[*]This is an updated version of a reading copyrighted in 1973 by Richard D. Irwin, Inc., Homewood, Illinois, as a chapter in the third edition of *The Life and Health Insurance Handbook,* edited by Davis W. Gregg and Vane B. Lucas. All rights reserved. This material or parts thereof may not be reproduced in any form without permission of the publisher.
[†]Fred J. Dopheide, JD, CLU, is a retired vice president, Educational Resources, the American Society of CLU & ChFC, Bryn Mawr, Pennsylvania.

for purposes of exclusion from income tax, includes death benefits payable under accident and health insurance contracts as well as workers' compensation insurance,[2] but does not include death benefits payable under an annuity contract.

Interest Option

When death proceeds are held by the insurer for future withdrawal or distribution and only interest on the proceeds is paid to the beneficiary, the full interest payment is taxable.[3]

Installment Options

For policies that matured by death before August 17, 1954, proceeds distributed under policy settlement options are fully tax free even though each payment contains an interest element. For policies maturing by death after August 16, 1954, that portion of each payment made under the fixed-period, fixed-amount, or life income installment options representing the principal of death proceeds is received tax free, but that portion representing interest is taxable. To calculate the taxable portion, the lump-sum death benefit that could have been received tax free is prorated over the payment period of the option, and the portion of each payment representing principal is tax free. The remainder representing interest is reportable as ordinary income.[4] In this calculation, the *payment period of the option* must be determined. Where the fixed-period option is in operation, the payment period is the number of guaranteed annual installments; where the fixed-amount option is in operation, it is the number of annual installments of a specified amount produced under the guaranteed interest rate in the policy; and, under the life income option, the payment period is the life expectancy of the beneficiary. (If the life income option has a refund or period-certain feature, the present value of such feature must be subtracted from the lump-sum death proceeds before proration.) Life expectancy and valuation of refund features are determined on the basis of mortality tables prescribed by the Secretary of the Treasury in the regulations.[5]

Interest Exclusion

With respect to deaths of insureds occurring before October 23, 1986, a surviving spouse-beneficiary may still exclude from income up to $1,000 of interest payable under a settlement option, but only where the option is installment in nature; that is, if the payments are a true combination of both interest and principal. This special interest exclusion has been repealed for deaths occurring after October 22, 1986.[6]

Qualified Accelerated Death Benefits

In 1992, the IRS issued proposed regulations regarding the treatment of certain accelerated death benefits under a life insurance contract. In these proposed regulations, the IRS stated that it will allow accelerated death benefits paid under a life insurance contract to be treated as amounts paid by reason of the death of the insured, and therefore excludible from gross income, if certain requirements are met. The most important requirement is that the insured be terminally ill in order for an accelerated death benefit to be excludible. Under the regulations, the insured is "terminally ill" if he or she has an illness that is reasonably expected to result in death within 12 months of the payment of the benefit, notwithstanding appropriate medical care. Final regulations have not been promulgated as of this writing.[7]

Life Insurance Living Benefits

Policy in Force

Prior to the Tax Reform Act of 1984, any increase in the cash value of a policy was not taxable, because a taxpayer's right to receive such income was subject to substantial limitations. A taxpayer did not have constructive receipt of increases, because to receive the gain he or she must have surrendered the policy and forfeited his or her rights.[8] Today, of course, many permanent life insurance policies permit withdrawals without policy termination. However, tax-deferred buildup of internal policy values is still allowed if the insurance policy meets certain actuarial tests. If these tests are not met, then the policy will be treated as a combination of term life insurance and a currently taxable fund.

Dividends are generally not taxable income but are viewed as a return of a portion of the premium, whether they are received in cash, used to either reduce or purchase additional coverage, or left with the company.[9] However, if aggregate dividends received or credited exceed the taxpayer's cost basis in the contract, such excess is taxable as ordinary income.[10] Interest earned on dividend accumulations is taxable in the year the taxpayer has the right to withdraw the interest. The taxpayer has constructive receipt of the interest income whether or not the income is withdrawn.

Withdrawals of cash value from a life policy are generally taxed on a first-in first-out (FIFO) basis; that is, withdrawals are treated as a nontaxable return of capital to the extent of premiums paid. Withdrawals in excess of premiums paid are taxable.

However, it is critically important to understand that withdrawals will be taxed as income first (a last-in first-out (LIFO) treatment) if the policy is classified as a modified endowment contract (MEC). The MEC rules are discussed in detail in the next reading in this book.

In addition, withdrawals from a universal life policy that are made during the first 15 policy years and are associated with a reduction in the policy's death benefit will also be subject to LIFO tax treatment, even if the policy is not a MEC.

Lump-Sum Payments

Where the owner of a life insurance contract receives the lifetime maturity proceeds or cash surrender value of the policy in one lump-sum payment, the amount received in excess of the owner's cost basis is subject to ordinary income tax.[11] Cost basis is defined as the investment in the contract, which is the sum of premiums paid, less policy dividends actually received, less any policy loans,[12] less extra premiums paid for certain supplementary benefits, such as waiver of premium and accidental death protection.[13]

Gain realized upon surrender or maturity of United States Government Life Insurance (WW I) or National Service Life Insurance (WW II) is exempt from tax.[14]

No loss is recognized where, upon maturity or surrender, the amount received is less than the cost basis. The difference represents the cost of pure insurance protection—a nondeductible expense.

When the owner of a life insurance contract sells the policy to a third party, such a transaction is not considered a *sale or exchange* for income tax purposes. Thus the gain in such a transaction is taxed as ordinary income and not as capital gain.[15] Any gain is taxable as ordinary income and is determined in the same way as it would be upon surrender of the contract.

Interest Option

Where the policyowner leaves maturity or cash surrender values with the insurance company under the interest-only option, the interest earned will be taxable as ordinary income when received or credited to the payee.[16] In addition, at the time of maturity or surrender, if the values available to the policyowner exceed the cost basis, the gain will be taxed as ordinary income even though the lifetime proceeds are left with the insurance company, *provided* the policyowner also reserves the right to withdraw the proceeds at any time.[17] This right of withdrawal places the policyowner in constructive receipt of the gain. To avoid constructive receipt and thereby postpone the tax on any gain, the policyowner must elect the interest option *before* maturity or surrender and give up give up the right to withdraw the proceeds.[18] In such a case, the person who ultimately receives the proceeds will bear the tax liability for the gain.

Installment Options

When the policyowner places maturity or cash surrender values under any of the installment options, the annuity provisions of the Internal Revenue Code apply.[19] Part of each installment payment is considered a return of principal and is not subject to tax. The percentage of each installment received tax free is found by dividing the investment in the contract by the expected total return.[20] The Code provides a "60-day rule"[21] that affects the definition of "investment in the contract." The rule has significance when, at the time of maturity or surrender, the lifetime proceeds exceed the owner's cost basis. The rule enables the policyowner to avoid immediate tax on the gain, but as a result a larger percentage of the installment payments will be subject to tax. The rule works this way: If the policyowner elects the installment option no later than 60 days following the date of maturity or surrender of the policy, there will be no tax on the unrealized gain until installments begin and *investment in the contract* will be the aggregate of premiums paid less dividends, loans, and premiums for certain supplementary benefits.[22] If, on the other hand, the owner delays electing the installment option until beyond the 60-day period, the owner will be taxed on the total unrealized gain as of the time of maturity or surrender, but the investment in the contract will be increased to the total maturity or surrender value, thus enlarging the tax-free portion of future installments. This will be accomplished, however, at the expense of exposing the total gain on the contract to taxation in one year.

Where the option selected is the life income option, the *investment in the contract* is reduced by the actuarial value of any refund or period-certain feature.[23]

The expected total return under the fixed-period option is determined by multiplying the fixed number of years or months by the amount of the guaranteed payment provided in the contract for such period.[24] Under the fixed-amount option, the expected total return is determined by multiplying the fixed-installment amount by the number of guaranteed installments.[25] Under the life income option, the expected return is determined by multiplying the periodic payment by the payee's life expectancy as determined by government tables.[26]

Contingent Beneficiaries

Where the primary payee dies before receiving all installments under the fixed-period or fixed-amount options, the contingent beneficiary will be taxed in the same manner as was the primary payee. That is, the contingent beneficiary will exclude the same portion of each installment from income and include the same portion of each installment in income.[27] However, where the primary payee is receiving a life income settlement and dies during a period of guaranteed payments, the contingent beneficiary will have no taxable income until the total amount received, when added to the amount that was received tax free by the primary payee, exceeds the investment in the contract.[28] Thereafter the full amount of each payment will be taxed as ordinary income.

Health Insurance Benefits

Disability Income Payments

Disability income insurance can be provided as a rider to a life insurance policy or through a separate contract. In either event, income payments on policies owned and paid for by the insured are received by the insured tax free.[29] When payments are made to a policyowner other than the insured—for example, to a corporation that has purchased the disability income insurance as key person insurance—the benefits paid by the insurance company continue to be tax free.[30]

A different situation arises, however, where disability income insurance is paid for by an employer to fund a wage continuation plan for employees, and the benefits are paid by the insurance company directly to the individual employees. Upon receipt of disability income from such a policy, an employee must include amounts received under the policy in income.

Medical Reimbursement

Benefits payable from hospital and surgical policies, major medical policies, and other insured medical expense coverages, whether from an individual or nondiscriminatory group policy, are exempt from income tax.[31] However, any benefits received must be used to reduce the amount of related medical expenses otherwise deductible for the year. In addition, to the extent that reimbursement is received for medical expenses taken as a tax deduction in a prior year, it will be taxable in the current year.

Income Tax Treatment Of Premiums

Personal Life Insurance

The general rule with respect to the income tax treatment of life insurance premiums is that they are a personal expense and as such are not deductible.[32] The rule applies whether the premium is paid by the insured, the beneficiary, or the policyowner. Exceptions to the general rule exist in certain situations based upon the use to which the life insurance is put. Examples include premiums paid by a business creditor for insurance purchased as collateral security for the debt, premiums paid for life insurance owned by a qualified charitable organization, premiums paid for life insurance by an ex-spouse as part of an alimony decree, and premiums paid by a business for life insurance used to fund certain employee benefit plans.

Business Life Insurance

Generally premiums paid on business life insurance are not deductible. The Internal Revenue Code is explicit: "No deduction shall be allowed for . . . premiums paid on any life insurance policy covering the life of any officer or employee, or of any person financially interested in any trade or business carried on by the taxpayer, when the taxpayer is directly or indirectly a beneficiary under such policy."[33] Premiums on business life insurance have been characterized by the Internal Revenue Service as a capital investment and not a business expense, even though the policy is term insurance.[34]

Personal Health Insurance

Prior to 1967 the question of whether personal disability income premiums were a deductible medical expense led to considerable litigation. Eventually the Internal Revenue Code was amended to provide that premiums paid for personal disability income insurance are not deductible.[35] Included in the definition of disability income insurance are policies that pay a weekly income payment to the insured while hospitalized.[36]

Premiums paid for medical reimbursement insurance are considered a medical care expense under the Code[37] and are deductible to the extent that they, along with other itemized medical expenses, exceed 7.5 percent of the taxpayer's adjusted gross income.

Business Health Insurance

Where an employer pays premiums on a disability income policy on the life of an employee and benefits are payable to the employer, no premium deduction is allowable,[38] but benefits are received tax free. This tax treatment is similar to key person life insurance owned by a business on a key employee.

However, where the employer pays premiums on disability income insurance with benefits paid directly to the employees under a wage continuation plan, such premiums are deductible by the employer and are not taxable to the covered employee,[39] provided such premium payments, when added to all other compensation paid to the covered employees, do not exceed a reasonable allowance for personal services rendered.[40]

Premiums paid by an employer on a policy providing medical reimbursement to the employee are deductible to the employer and are not taxable to the employee,[41] if they meet the test of reasonableness and are part of an employee benefit plan.[42]

LIFE INSURANCE ARRANGEMENTS GIVING RISE TO TAX CONSEQUENCES

Transfer for Value

Perhaps the most prominent exception to the general rule that life insurance death proceeds are tax exempt is the transfer-for-value rule.[43] Where a policy transferred by assignment or otherwise for a valuable consideration matures by reason of death, the transferee will be liable for income tax on the amount of death proceeds in excess of the actual value of the consideration paid for the contract plus the total of net premiums subsequently paid by the transferee.[44] This rule, which seems to be deeply grounded in public policy, is designed to prevent a tax-free windfall that might come about from speculation in life insurance policies. Life insurance enjoys an income-tax-favored position because of its unique economic function of protecting families and business interests that would profit more by the insured's continued life than by death. Therefore one who buys life insurance policies for speculation with the hope of realizing a substantial monetary profit on the death of the insured will not enjoy a tax exemption.

However, Congress did recognize that certain transfers of life insurance for consideration are not motivated by a desire for profit but for valid personal or business reasons. Therefore Congress included five exceptions in the Code to the transfer-for-value rule.[45] When any one of these exceptions applies, the full death proceeds will be income tax free in the hands of the beneficiary even though the policy was transferred for a valuable consideration.

The five specified exceptions are (1) transfers to the insured, (2) transfers to a partner of the insured, (3) transfers to a partnership in which the insured is a partner, (4) transfers to a corporation in which the insured is a shareholder or an officer, and (5) transfers in which the transferee's basis in the transferred policy is determined in whole or in part by reference to the transferor's basis. This latter exception (occasionally referred to as the *carryover-basis* exception) would apply in a tax-free exchange, where, for example, one corporation transfers a corporate-owned key person policy to another corporation in a tax-free reorganization. The carryover-basis exception may also apply where a policy is transferred in a part-sale/part-gift transaction.[46] In part-sale/part-gift transfers the basis of the property transferred in the hands of the transferee is determined by reference to the transferor's basis where the amount paid by the transferee for the property is less than the transferor's adjusted basis in the property.[47] This exception also applies to transfers of policies between spouses incident to a divorce, since such transfers are nontaxable.[48]

It is worthwhile to reflect on the conspicuous absence in the Code of other transfer situations that are not excepted and yet may be motivated by personal or business reasons that are equally as valid as those surrounding the exceptions enumerated in the Code. One can think of many family transfers that would not involve speculation but would be made for sound estate planning reasons. One glaring omission is the transfer of a policy from an insured who is a shareholder in a closely held corporation to a fellow shareholder. As in the transfer of a policy from a partner-insured to a fellow partner, there may be sound business reasons for such a transfer, yet the rule excepts the latter but not the former. Conscientious planners need to be especially mindful of these nonexceptions.

The tax results of a transfer-for-value problem can be onerous. Because of the aleatory nature of a life insurance contract, the amount exposed to ordinary income in one year can be substantial. Thus careful attention must be paid to every transfer of a life insurance policy in order to avoid the tax pitfall of the transfer-for-value rule. Examples of transfers that are not uncommon but that violate the rule include the following:

- A policyowner sells a policy on his or her life to a corporation in which he or she is an employee and/or member of the board of directors. (The insured must be a shareholder or officer.)
- Alice and Bruce own all the stock of a corporation and enter into a buy-sell agreement on a cross-purchase basis. Instead of buying new life insurance on each other's lives to fund the agreement, Alice and Bruce each transfer to the other an existing policy on their lives. (Coshareholders are not exempt transferees.)
- The Alice-Bruce Corporation has a stock redemption agreement with Alice and Bruce funded with corporate-owned insurance on Alice and Bruce. The parties wish to change the stock retirement arrangement to a cross-purchase plan. The corporation transfers Alice's policy to Bruce and Bruce's policy to Alice.

The above transactions are clearly transfers for value subject to tax at the death of the insured. Planning techniques may be available to achieve the desired results without falling into the transfer-for-value "trap." Other more subtle situations may bring the rule into play. In some instances the parties may be unaware that a transfer is being made or of the consideration involved.

For example, assume that corporate owners, Alice and Bruce, enter into a cross-purchase buy-sell arrangement and elect to fund it with group life insurance—a procedure not normally recommended. Alice, on her group certificate, names Bruce as beneficiary; and Bruce, on his certificate, names Alice as beneficiary. Alice and Bruce may not be consciously aware that they are transferring anything to each other, but the broad definition of "transfer for a valuable consideration" given in the regulations seems to suggest that Alice and Bruce are transferees for value:

> . . . a "transfer for a valuable consideration" is any absolute transfer for value of the right to receive all or a part of the proceeds of a life insurance policy. Thus the creation, for value, of an enforceable contractual right to receive all or a part of the proceeds of a policy may constitute a transfer for a valuable consideration of the policy or an interest therein.[49]

Thus it might be argued that Alice and Bruce have transferred for consideration an interest in their group life insurance to each other. The consideration seems to consist of reciprocal promises to fund their business agreement with cross-beneficiary designations.

A policy that has been transferred for value can be cleansed of the taint by a subsequent transfer of the policy, for value or otherwise, to an exempt transferee; for example, the insured.[50] However, the transfer-for-value taint is not removed by a subsequent gift of the policy to a nonexempt transferee. Thus where Robert, the insured, sells his $10,000 policy to Stanley, his son, for $3,000 and Stanley then gives the policy to his sister, Dawn, the policy is still subject to the transfer-for-value rule. At the insured's death, the proceeds in excess of $3,000, plus premiums paid subsequent to the transfer to Stanley, will be subject to ordinary income tax.[51]

Lack of Insurable Interest

The concept of insurable interest has had an influence on the taxation of life insurance proceeds. Lacking the requisite of insurable interest, life insurance has been viewed as a mere wagering contract entered into for profit. This was the view of the court in a case[52] where a corporation paid the premium on accidental death insurance on its truck drivers, with the corporation named as beneficiary of the death proceeds. When a driver was killed, the proceeds collected by the corporation were held to be profits subject to ordinary income tax. It was the view of the court that the truck driver was not a key person and that the corporation did not at any time have an insurable interest in the truck driver's life. The decision reminds us that the question of insurable interest in a business insurance situation is one that continues to merit careful attention.

In an earlier case[53] the Tax Court went so far as to tax the proceeds of a key person policy where an insurable interest existed at the inception of the contract but presumably not when the policy matured as a death claim. On appeal, however, the U.S. Court of Appeals for the Sixth Circuit reversed and held that the proceeds were not taxable for lack of an insurable interest. The court pointed out that local law required an insurable interest only at the time of inception of the contract. The requirement of insurable interest generally applies only at the time of policy inception.

It is possible for a business to have an insurable interest in a key person who is not an employee. In one Tax Court decision,[54] the IRS argued that key person life insurance proceeds received by a corporation on the life of an independent contractor were taxable as ordinary income. But the Tax Court disagreed, holding that the insured's services as a real estate developer were essential to the success of the corporation and that the corporation had a valid insurable interest in the real estate developer's life. As a result, the tax-free nature of the death proceeds was preserved. The question of insurable interest is important and should be considered at policy inception.

Proceeds as Corporate Distributions

If business life insurance is arranged so that proceeds of policies that are owned and paid for by a corporation are paid to beneficiaries other than the corporation, complex tax problems will arise. For example, when the beneficiaries are shareholders of the corporation they may think the proceeds paid directly to them by the life insurance company retain their tax-free character. The IRS has refused to accept this point of view, maintaining instead that such insurance proceeds are taxable as dividends because the result is the same as if the proceeds had been received tax free as life insurance proceeds by the corporation and then distributed to the shareholder as a dividend.[55] The IRS's position has the logical advantage, and this was acknowledged in at least one case.[56] Therefore in situations where a corporation owns and pays for life insurance to fund a buy-sell arrangement or to protect the corporation against the loss of a key employee, the corporation, and not the shareholders, should be the beneficiary.[57]

A collateral problem raised by unorthodox business insurance arrangements is taxability of the premiums. If a corporation pays premiums on business life insurance where shareholders are beneficiaries, or where shareholders are beneficiaries as well as owners of the life insurance, the premiums are taxable to the shareholders as dividends.[58]

An earlier assignment discussed the three types of losses that are deductible to an individual: (1) losses incurred in a trade or business, (2) losses incurred in a transaction entered into for profit, and (3) casualty losses. Section 165 of the Code generally allows deductions for such losses provided they are "not compensated by insurance or otherwise." The quoted language has been interpreted by the Tax Court in the *Johnson* case to include the death proceeds of life insurance. Therefore where a taxpayer purchased life insurance on the life of a partner to protect the investment in the partnership, and in fact such a loss was incurred on the partner's death, a loss deduction under Section 165 was disallowed because, according to the Tax Court, the life insurance proceeds compensated for the loss.[59]

The result in the *Johnson* case normally should not present a tax problem for businesses obtaining key person life insurance protection to provide funds to find a replacement or to fund a 303 stock redemption, a salary continuation arrangement, or a stock purchase or partnership purchase plan. The *Johnson* case will hopefully be applied as a precedent only in similar cases, namely, when the key person life insurance is specifically obtained to protect the surviving partner's investment in the partnership. There is a clear and direct link between an anticipated Section 165 loss and the acquisition of life insurance to compensate that loss—a link that is not normally associated with the acquisition of key person life insurance.

Credit-Debtor Situations

Life insurance serves a valuable commercial function in the extension of credit. The security against death provided by a life insurance policy may mean the difference between a loan being granted or not being granted. But what are the tax consequences of life insurance used in this setting?

Before examining the tax aspects, it might be helpful to keep in focus the gradations of life insurance arrangements possible where a creditor wishes life insurance security. Perhaps the simplest arrangement is for the insured-debtor to use an existing policy and simply name the creditor as beneficiary. Although this is the simplest method, it would hardly satisfy most creditors. The next possibility is to have the insured-debtor effect a collateral assignment of an existing policy to the creditor. The insured would still pay the premiums, and the creditor would have certain rights in the policy that would terminate upon satisfaction of the debt. Conceivably the creditor could pay the premiums in these instances, but practically the creditor would only pay premiums if the debtor was unable to do so. The next gradation would be a policy on the insured-debtor with full ownership rights in the creditor, with the creditor named as beneficiary. The creditor might or might not pay the premiums.

Deductibility of Premiums

Where the debtor owns the policy on his or her life and pays the premiums, it seems quite clear that the premiums are not deductible.[60] This is true even where the debtor is required to provide life insurance in order to obtain the loan. The same rule of nondeductibility applies where the debtor assigns a personally owned policy to the creditor as collateral security, and the debtor continues to pay the premiums. The courts have held that the insured, in paying premiums, is buying a personal benefit because the purchase of the policy enables the insured to obtain a loan. In addition, the insured's estate would benefit because the debt would be eliminated upon death. For these reasons the premiums constitute personal, nondeductible expenses.

Where the debtor owns the policy and collaterally assigns it to a business creditor to secure the debt and the creditor pays the premiums, deductibility of the premium payment may apply in special circumstances. The position of the IRS is that the premiums are deductible only if (1) the creditor has a right to reimbursement for premiums paid (whether express or implied), and (2) such right is worthless in the taxable year in question.[61] Assuming that the policy involved was term insurance and that the debtor was insolvent, it would seem that the creditor would be entitled to a business bad-debt deduction for the amount of the debt including premiums paid. Further, if the creditor continued to pay premiums on the assigned policy, continuing premium payments would be deductible. The same rule applies where the policy has cash values, provided the amount of the loan is greater than the cash surrender value.[62] The premium deduction is allowable to the business creditor as an ordinary and necessary business expense incident to the need of the creditor to protect its collateral by keeping the policy in force. It is well to remember, however, that the rule of premium deductibility by a business creditor applies only where the debtor is insolvent.

In a situation where the business creditor applies for, owns, and pays the premiums for a policy on the debtor's life, one can be more positive regarding the deductibility of the premiums. An old ruling of the IRS[63] granted a deduction to the creditor but limited it to the excess of premiums over cash surrender value, presumably that portion of the annual premium that exceeded the cash value increase for the year in question. A more recent Revenue Ruling[64] states that if the policies purchased and owned by the business creditor are term life insurance policies with amounts of insurance that do not exceed the unpaid balance of the debt, then the creditor's premium payments are fully deductible as ordinary and necessary business expenses. In determining whether premiums paid for insurance on the life of a debtor to secure the debt are deductible, key questions concerning policy ownership, premium payer, and amount and type of insurance need to be answered.

Example: Sherry borrows $100,000 from Gina, a business creditor, to start her own business. Gina is concerned about whether Sherry can repay the money. Therefore Gina applies for a term policy with a face amount of $50,000 on the life of Sherry. Gina pays the premiums on the policy. So long as the outstanding principal balance of the loan from Gina to Sherry is $50,000 or more, Gina may deduct in full the premiums on the $50,000 term policy.

Death Proceeds

The proceeds of life insurance on the life of a debtor received by a creditor are not tax exempt as life insurance proceeds. They are received as a collection of the unpaid balance of the debt rather than "by death of the insured," as the language is used within the meaning of Section 101(a).[65] Proceeds received to the extent of the outstanding debt are tax free as a return of capital unless the creditor has previously taken a bad-debt deduction, in which case the proceeds so received must be included in gross income.[66] Any premium amounts that have been deducted by the creditor and later recovered as proceeds must be reported as taxable income.[67] Any amount of proceeds representing interest on the debt are taxed as ordinary income to the creditor.[68] Should the creditor receive amounts in excess of the outstanding debt, premiums paid, and other amounts owing to the creditor, it would seem that such *excess* proceeds would still not be tax exempt because of the important question of insurable interest. This might be the case in creditor-owned life insurance originally purchased and owned by the creditor, as distinguished from collaterally assigned life insurance or even absolutely assigned life insurance where, in most states, the creditor's recovery of proceeds is limited to the amount of the debt plus the premiums paid, interest, and other expenses, with any excess deemed to be held by the creditor as a constructive trustee for the benefit of the named beneficiary or estate of the insured.

Charitable Contribution

Premiums paid on life insurance owned by a qualified charitable organization are deductible to the donor as a charitable contribution, subject to the charitable contributions limitations.[69] It is important that the charity be the owner of the policy and have the exclusive right to cash in the policy, borrow on it, or change the beneficiary.

One technique for achieving deductibility of life insurance premiums that is occasionally suggested is simply to name the charity as irrevocable beneficiary of the policy proceeds. This technique should be avoided because it is fraught with uncertainties. We know that the irrevocable beneficiary is given some ownership interest in the policy, but the exact nature is frequently clouded, especially in the area of charitable giving. Perhaps, more importantly, the Internal Revenue Code denies a charitable deduction for gifts to charities where less than the taxpayer's entire interest in the property is contributed.[70] The Code enumerates certain exceptions that do not seem to encompass partial gifts of life insurance.[71]

Separation and Divorce

Income tax consequences need to be considered carefully where life insurance is involved in separation agreements and divorce decrees.

Life Insurance in the Property Settlement

The transfer of property between husband and wife incident to a divorce is generally nontaxable. The spouse who receives the property has a carryover basis and pays income tax on appreciation if the property is sold. This means that there is no taxable event with respect to cash values when life insurance is transferred as a result of a divorce.

Premium Payments

Premium payments by one spouse[72] or former spouse for life insurance owned by and benefiting the other spouse are deductible as alimony by the payer-spouse under Section 215 of the Code and taxable to the payee-spouse under Section 71 of the Code if the following occurs:

- Payments are made in cash and terminate at the death of the payee-spouse.
- Payments are made under a divorce decree or separation agreement.
- The parties are not members of the same household and do not file joint tax returns.
- Payments are not for child support.
- Payments must be made for at least 3 years unless either spouse dies or the payee-spouse remarries.

Death Proceeds

Prior to the Tax Reform Act of 1984 life insurance proceeds on the life of one spouse were not tax exempt when paid to the other spouse to discharge legal obligations imposed by a divorce decree, separation agreement, or support decree. Under current law, it is safe to assume that such life insurance proceeds are exempt from income tax.

Additional Compensation

Where the employee is the policyowner and the employer has no beneficial interest in the policy, premium payments by an employer on an individual policy insuring the life of an employee may be deductible by the employer.

Such an arrangement is often referred to as an "informal pension plan," whereby an employer selects certain favored employees for this nonqualified fringe benefit. The employee applies for the policy and possesses all incidents of ownership. The employee names his or her own personal beneficiary for the death benefit, and the employer pays the annual premium. Such payment, if considered reasonable additional compensation to the employee for services rendered, will be deductible under Section 162 of the Code as an ordinary and necessary business expense.[73] An important element in the success of this arrangement is that the payments must qualify as additional compensation and not as dividends should the employee also be a shareholder. It is also important that the total amount of compensation realized by the employee, including the premium payment, meet the test of reasonableness. Finally, the employer must not be a beneficiary of the policy, either directly or indirectly.[74]

Such premium payments by the employer are taxable to the employee when paid. The questions are often asked, Why arrange such a plan? Wouldn't it be equally effective if the employer simply increased the employee's salary by the amount of the premium and let the employee buy the life insurance with the increase in salary? It is true that the same tax result would follow, but whether the effect would be equal is the question to ponder. The employer has an opportunity to place himself or herself in a psychologically advantageous position by selecting one or more *key employees* for the benefit *plan*. The package of benefits embodied in a life insurance contract such as a substantial death benefit, disability features, and lifetime guaranteed retirement income may be more appreciated by an employee (and especially by the family) than a nominal salary increase to cover the premium payment.

Split-Dollar Life Insurance

A popular fringe benefit for selected employees is the split-dollar life insurance plan. Under a typical split-dollar arrangement, an employee and employer share or *split* the premium payments. Cash-value-type policies are universally used with the employer's share of the annual premium being measured by each year's increase in cash value. The employee's share of each premium payment is generally the difference between each year's cash value increase and the amount of net premium due. The employer is named beneficiary to the extent of the cash value, and the employee has the right to name his or her own beneficiary for the difference between the total death proceeds payable and the cash value.

Under such a plan an employee receives a substantial amount of life insurance at a relatively low cost. The employer pays the major share of each premium (at some point in the life of the policy, the employer may be paying *all* the premium) and thus bestows an economic benefit on the employee.[75] The employee thus must include in gross income each year the value of the economic benefit received, which is measured by the government's P.S. 58 rates.[76] The value of the employee's economic benefit each year is determined by multiplying the applicable P.S. 58 rate at the employee's age by the amount of net death protection provided that year. The employee's part of the premium paid for that year (if any) may be subtracted from the total value of the economic benefit taxable to the employee.

No deduction is available to the employer for contributions to a split-dollar plan[77] because the employer is also a beneficiary under such policy within the meaning of Section 264(a)(1) of the Code.

There are several different variations of split-dollar arrangements. Some are quite sophisticated. The individual circumstances of both the employer and employee must be considered in determining the features of a particular plan.

SUMMARY

Although death proceeds of life insurance enjoy shelter from the impact of federal income tax in the vast majority of instances, the very nature of life insurance as valuable property as well as its flexibility in solving human problems has led to its imaginative use in business and personal situations where careful planning is required to avoid income tax pitfalls. Thus all proposed transfers of life insurance should be closely examined to avoid transfer-for-value problems; the requirement of insurable interest should be taken into account as a tax-oriented dimension of concern; the proper arrangement of policy ownership and beneficiary designation should be given thorough consideration where premiums are paid with corporate dollars; and the disposition or use of life insurance in separation and divorce cases should be accomplished with specialized guidance to avoid unfavorable tax results.

The questions of life insurance premium deductibility and taxation are of special concern in insured-debtor situations, in charitable giving, and in planning life insurance fringe benefits for selected employees. Again, in these complicated yet common transactions, the desired tax results can be accomplished best through an awareness of the tax principles involved.

NOTES

1. IRC Sec. 101(a)(1).
2. Treas. Reg. Sec. 1.101-1.
3. IRC Sec. 101(c).
4. IRC Sec. 101(d)(1).
5. P.L. 99-514, Tax Reform Act of 1986, Sec. 1001(b).
6. P.L. 99-514, Tax Reform Act of 1986, Sec. 1001(a).
7. Prop. Reg. Sec. 1.7702-2(d).

8. *Griffith v. United States,* 360 F.2d 210 (CA 3, 1966), affirming 245 F. Supp. 678 (1965).
9. IRC Sec. 72(d)(1)(B); Treas. Reg. Sec. 1.72-11(b)(1).
10. Ibid.
11. IRC Sec. 72(e).
12. Treas. Reg. Sec. 1.72-6(a)(1).
13. Rev. Rul. 55-349, 1955-1 C.B. 232.
14. 38 USC Sec. 3101(a).
15. *Commissioner v. Phillips,* 275 F.2d 33 (CA 4, 1960).
16. IRC Sec. 72(j).
17. Treas. Reg. Sec. 1.451-2; *Blum v. Higgins,* 150 F.2d 471 (CA 6, 1945).
18. *Constance C. Frackelton,* 46 B.T.A. 883, acq. C.B. 1944, p. 10.
19. IRC Sec. 72(a).
20. IRC Sec. 72(b).
21. IRC Sec. 72(h)(2).
22. Treas. Reg. Sec. 1.72-12.
23. IRC Sec. 72(c).
24. Treas. Reg. Sec. 1.72-5(c).
25. Treas. Reg. Sec. 1.72-5(d).
26. Treas. Reg. Sec. 1.72-5(a).
27. Treas. Reg. Sec. 1.72-11(c)(1)(2), Example 4.
28. Treas. Reg. Sec. 1.72-11(c)(1)(2), Example 1.
29. IRC Sec. 104(a)(3).
30. *Castner Garage, Ltd.,* 43 B.T.A. 1, acq. (1935).
31. IRC Sec. 105(b).
32. Treas. Reg. Sec. 1.262-1(b)(1).
33. IRC Sec. 264(a)(1).
34. OD 699 C.B. 3, 1261.
35. IRC Sec. 213(d)(1).
36. Rev. Rul. 68-451, 1968-2, C.B. 111.
37. IRC Sec. 213(d)(1)(C).
38. Rev. Rul. 66-262, 1966-2 C.B. 105.
39. IRC Sec. 106.
40. IRC Sec. 162(a)(1).
41. IRC Sec. 106.
42. Treas. Reg. Sec. 1.162-10(a).
43. IRC Sec. 101(a)(2).
44. Treas. Reg. Sec. 1.101-1(b).
45. IRC Sec. 101(a)(2)(A)(B).
46. Rev. Rul. 69-187, 1969-16 I.R.B. 8.
47. "Where a transfer of property is in part a sale and in part a gift, the unadjusted basis of the property in the hands of the transferee is the sum of—(1) Whichever of the following is the greater: (i) the amount paid by the transferee for the property, or (ii) the transferor's adjusted basis for the property at the time of the transfer . . ." Treas. Reg. Sec. 1.1015-4(a).
48. IRC Sec. 1041.

49. Treas. Reg. Sec. 1.101-1(b)(4).
50. Treas. Reg. Sec. 1.101-1(b)(3).
51. See citation in footnote 49, *supra.*
52. *Atlantic Oil v. Patterson,* 331 F.2d 516 (CA 5, 1964).
53. *Francis H. W. Ducros,* 272 F.2d 49 (CA 6, 1959).
54. *M. Lucille Harrison,* 59 T.C. No. 57 (1973).
55. Rev. Rul. 61-134, I.R.B. 1961-2.
56. *Golden v. Commissioner,* 113 F.2d 590 (CA 3, 1940); Rev. Rul. 71-79, I.R.B. 1971-7, 17. But see *Estate of J. E. Horne,* 63 T.C. No. 98 (1975), acq. in result, 1980-1 C.B. 1, where proceeds payable to a shareholder on a corporate-owned policy were held not to be dividends where the proceeds could also be included in the gross estate of the deceased for federal estate tax purposes by Treas. Reg. Sec. 20.2042-1(c)(6). The *Horne* case is perhaps an aberration. Its result was a unique attempt by the court to achieve a degree of equity between conflicting ownership concepts. Although in fact the corporation owned the life insurance policy, the Treasury's own estate tax regulations attributed ownership to the insured. In a 1981 Technical Advice Memorandum (LTR 8144001), the IRS took the position that when the death proceeds of a corporate-owned life insurance policy on a majority shareholder were paid to the deceased shareholder's spouse, the proceeds were excludible under IRC Sec. 101(a) because the beneficiary spouse was not a shareholder.
57. Where the insured is a controlling shareholder of a corporation, life insurance on the insured's life owned by the corporation but payable other than for the benefit of the corporation will be includible in its entirety in the estate of the insured for federal estate tax purposes. Treas. Reg. Sec. 20.2042-1(c)(6).
58. Rev. Rul. 59-184, 1959-1 C.B. 65.
59. *A. N. Johnson,* 66 T.C. 897, (1976), aff'd. 78-1 USTC (CA-4, 1978). When the insured partner died, the surviving partner claimed a capital loss on liquidation of the partnership. It was this loss that the court held as compensated for by life insurance. The surviving partner argued unsuccessfully that (1) the life insurance compensated him for the loss of his partner's life, not for the loss of his investment in the partnership; (2) IRC Sec. 165 does not apply to life insurance; (3) unlike casualty insurance, the payment of life insurance death proceeds is not dependent on an investment loss; and (4) the disallowance of his loss deduction had the effect of taxing the life insurance death proceeds in contravention of IRC Sec. 101(a).
60. *Glassner v. Commissioner,* 360 F.2d 33 (CA 3, 1966); *Klein v. Commissioner,* 84 F.2d 310 (CA 7, 1936).
61. Rev. Rul. 75-46, 1975-7 C.B. 8.
62. See citation in footnote 60.
63. OD 38, 1 C.B. 104 (1919). Obsolete Ruling list, Rev. Rul. 68-575, I.R.B. 1968-43, 31.
64. Rev. Rul. 70-254, I.R.B. 1970-21, 1970-1 C.B. 31.
65. Albeit death is a prerequisite to the fund coming into existence. Treas. Reg. Sec. 1.101-1(b)(4); *Landfield Finance Co. v. U.S.,* 418 F.2d 172 (CA 7, 1969).
66. *T.O. McCamant,* 32 T.C. 824.
67. *St. Louis Refrigerating and Cold Storage Co. v. U.S.,* 162 F.2d 394 (CA 8, 1947).
68. See citation in footnote 66, *supra.*
69. IRC Sec. 170; *Eppa Hunton IV,* 1 T.C. 821.
70. IRC Sec. 170(f)(3).

71. The IRS, in two Revenue Rulings, reinforced this view. Rev. Rul. 76-1, I.R.B. 1976-1, 8 denied a charitable deduction for premiums paid on "split-life" insurance and in Rev. Rul. 76-143, I.R.B. 1976-16, 9 deductibility was denied for split-dollar plan premiums. In each instance the charity had a partial ownership interest in the plan.

72. In an effort to achieve clarity in this discussion, it will be assumed that the male spouse is making alimony or support payments to the female spouse. IRC Secs. 71 and 215 make the same assumption and attendant regulations make clear that the Code sections equally apply to payments by an ex-wife to an ex-husband.

73. *Twin City Tile and Marble Co.,* 32 F.2d 229 (CA 8, 1929); *Hubert Transfer and Storage,* 7 T.C.M. 171; Treas. Reg. Sec. 1.61-2(d)(2)(ii)(a).

74. IRC Sec. 264(a); Rev. Rul. 70-148, I.R.B. 1970-14, 9; 1970-1 C.B. 60.

75. Rev. Rul. 64-328, 1964-2 C.B. 11.

76. The insurance company's one-year term rates may be used to measure the economic benefits, if lower than the P.S. 58 rates. Rev. Rul. 66-110, 1966-1 C.B. 12.

77. See citation in footnote 74, *supra.*

9

Income Tax Treatment of Modified Endowment Contracts*

Edward E. Graves and James F. Ivers III[†]

HISTORICAL PERSPECTIVE ON SINGLE-PREMIUM POLICIES

Single-premium life insurance policies experienced an 800 percent increase in sales volume between 1984 and 1988. This was mainly due to the Tax Reform Act of 1986, which eliminated many of the tax advantages of what had been popular tax-sheltered investments. After that legislation was enacted, many investors purchased single-premium life insurance policies. In many cases the income tax deferral was the primary motivation for the purchase. Some stock brokerages were promoting and selling single-premium life insurance policies as tax shelters. These policies were often described as the last remaining tax shelter under our tax law.

Single-premium life insurance policies and other limited pay policies enjoyed the same tax treatment as other life insurance policies (that is, cash-value buildup is generally income tax free until the policy is terminated). The policyowner was able to borrow against the policy in the form of policy loans and gain possession and management of the purchase price of the policy without being taxed.

CONGRESSIONAL ACTION

Members of Congress were disturbed by the marketing of single-premium life insurance. The Technical and Miscellaneous Revenue Act of 1988 (TAMRA '88) changed the income taxation of any policy entered into on or after June 21, 1988, that fails a test titled the *7-pay test* and consequently is classified a modified endowment contract (MEC).

Policies entered into *before* June 21, 1988, have been grandfathered and are not affected by this law unless they undergo a "material change." The material changes that can jeopardize the grandfather protection will be explained below.

*This reading is excerpted from *The Financial Services Professional's Guide to the State of the Art: 1989,* Stephan R. Leimberg et al. (Bryn Mawr, Pa.: The American College, 1989).
†Edward E. Graves, CLU, ChFC, is associate professor of insurance at The American College.

The objective of the changes in tax treatment for insurance policies classified as modified endowment contracts is to discourage the use of high-premium life insurance policies as short-term investments. This treatment makes the use of high-premium life insurance policies as short-term investments more costly and thereby decreases the return to the policyowner who takes possession of the cash value through loans, withdrawals, or terminations. However, the rules in no way decrease the return to policyowners who leave the funds with the insurer and look to the death benefit as the primary benefit of the contract.

The 7-Pay Test

The modified endowment contract rules affect the tax treatment of any policy entered into on or after June 21, 1988, in which the aggregate premiums paid at any time during the first 7 years of the contract exceed the sum of the "net level premiums" that would have been paid by that time if the contract provided for paid-up benefits after the payment of seven level annual premiums. This is called the *7-pay test.*

Policies that fail the 7-pay test because too much has been paid within the first 7 years are considered *modified endowment contracts* (MECs). For example, if the annual net level premium for a $100,000 7-pay policy is $4,500, then any $100,000 policy for the same insured on which aggregate premiums *exceed* $4,500 during the first year, $9,000 during the first 2 policy years, $13,500 during the first 3 policy years, $18,000 during the first 4 policy years, $22,500 during the first 5 policy years, $27,000 during the first 6 policy years, or $31,500 during the first 7 policy years will be considered a modified endowment contract.

If the aggregate premiums paid during the first 7 years are *equal to or less than* the aggregate premiums that would have been paid on a level-annual-premium basis using the net level premium amount ($4,500 a year in this example) for a 7-pay policy (for the same insured), the policy will *not* be a modified endowment contract and will receive the same tax treatment previously applicable to all policies.

The definition of a net level premium under these rules is based on the net single-premium concept under IRC Sec. 7702, which provides the definition of a life insurance contract. The net level premium is *not* the same as the actual premium payable under the contract. It is also not the same as what many life insurance professionals refer to as a net premium. "Net level premium" is a technical term of art created and defined by the tax law. Stated simply, however, net level premium is an artificially constructed amount based on reasonable mortality charges, an assumed interest rate, and (in some cases) reasonable insurance company expense charges. Therefore it is possible that even policies that require 7 level annual premiums in some cases will not pass the 7-pay test because the net level premium will be less than the actual premium. In other words, if the net level premium is less that the actual premium payable, the payment of the actual premium due will cause the policy to fail the 7-pay test.

Those policies entered into on or after June 21, 1988, that are classified as modified endowment contracts may be subjected to income taxes and penalty taxes not applicable to other life insurance policies. Policy loans and partial withdrawals of funds from such modified endowment contracts are subject to last-in first-out (LIFO) treatment to determine the applicable taxes. This means that any income earned on the contract fund is taxed as if it was withdrawn *before* the policyowner's cost basis in the contract. In addition to the regular income tax, a 10 percent penalty tax is generally applicable to any taxable gains withdrawn before the policyowner reaches age 59½. This includes policy terminations. However, the 10 percent penalty does not apply to payments attributable to disability or to annuitized payments.

> *Example:* Penelope purchased a life insurance contract on January 1, 1990. As of her 50th birthday, her basis in the policy is $100,000. The contract has a cash value of $140,000. The policy is a MEC. She borrows $50,000 from the policy's cash value on her 50th birthday. Penelope's taxable gain from the loan is $40,000 ($140,000 cash value−$100,000 basis in the policy). If Penelope is in the 36 percent tax bracket, she must pay an income tax of $14,400 ($40,000 x .36). She must also pay a 10 percent penalty on the taxable amount. The penalty will be $4,000 ($40,000 x .10). Therefore Penelope's total tax bill on the loan from the policy is $18,400 ($14,400 + $4,000).

Note that all amounts included in Penelope's gross income as a result of taking a loan from the policy are added to her basis in the policy for purposes of determining future taxable amounts. Therefore Penelope's basis in the policy after taking the loan will be $140,000 ($100,000 original basis + $40,000 taxable portion of loan). The $10,000 nontaxable portion does not affect Penelope's basis in the contract because the transaction is a loan and not a withdrawal.

These rules are similar to those applicable to deferred-annuity contracts issued after August 13, 1982. Income earned within such contracts is deemed to be withdrawn (and therefore taxable) before the cost basis of the contract is recovered when withdrawals are made before the annuity's starting date. However, life insurance policies that are not classified as modified endowment contracts, as well as so-called "pre-TEFRA" annuity contracts (those funded before August 14, 1982) are subject to a more favorable first-in first-out (FIFO) tax treatment on withdrawals.

Contracts with Death Benefits of $10,000 or Less

There is a variation on the application of the net level premium amount in the 7-pay test that applies to policies of $10,000 or less in face amount. The law provides an annual allowance of $75 to be added to the 7-pay test premium. The $75 additional allowance permits some small 7-pay policies to pass the 7-pay test when they otherwise might not. The smaller the policy is, the more likely it is that the actual premium will be less than the net level premium plus $75. The full $75 can be used for any amount of coverage between $1,000 and $10,000, resulting in a maximum allowable additional expense loading of $7.50 per $1,000 of coverage.

Congress anticipated the added attractiveness of this small policy expense allowance and its potential abuses. Therefore the statute requires that all policies issued by the same insurer to the same policyowner be treated as one policy for purposes of determining that the face amount does not exceed $10,000. This prevents policyowners from purchasing a large number of small policies to take advantage of the allowable expense loading. Note that the statute does not require that policies from *different* insurers be aggregated for this purpose. This may present a planning opportunity for taxpayers purchasing several small policies from different insurance companies.

Grandfathered Policies

Policies entered into prior to June 21, 1988 (as well as policies entered into on or after that date that pass the 7-pay test) will generally be treated the same as they have been in the past. There is no income tax applicable to withdrawals until after the cost basis has been recovered tax free. This is the first-in-first-out (FIFO) treatment long associated with life insurance policy taxation. Generally, no penalty tax is applicable to taxable gains from life insurance policies unless the policy is reclassified as a MEC.

It is important to remember that withdrawals from policies that are associated with a reduction in policy benefits during the first 15 policy years are currently subject to a limited LIFO-type federal income taxation. The MEC rules have been imposed *in addition to* these existing rules that were imposed by the Tax Reform Act of 1986. However, the 1986 rules do not apply to policy loans. The MEC rules do apply to loans as well as to withdrawals.

Subsequent Exchanges of a MEC

Once a policy is classified as a MEC, it will automatically make any policy subsequently received in exchange for it also a MEC. Even if the new policy received in the exchange passes the 7-pay test, it will be classified as a MEC.

Example: Merlin purchased a single-premium policy on August 1, 1990. The policy fails the 7-pay test and will be treated as a MEC. Merlin later exchanges his single-premium policy for a level premium whole life policy that clearly passes the 7-pay test. However, the new policy will be treated as a MEC because it was received in exchange for a MEC.

At first glance this appears to be a harsh result. However, Congress was apparently concerned about the potential for using untaxed internal policy gains to purchase additional life insurance coverage. In the absence of this provision a tax benefit similar to a deduction for premium payments would have existed.

MATERIAL CHANGE RULES

A policy that at first passes the 7-pay test when it is issued can later become a MEC if there is a "material change" in the policy. In addition, a single-premium policy entered into before June 21, 1988, is not a MEC but could become one if the policy is materially changed anytime after June 20, 1988, and fails the 7-pay test after the change.

What constitutes a material change under the MEC rules? An increase in future benefits under the contract will generally be considered a material change. However, the following will *not* be treated as material changes:

- cost-of-living increases in death benefits that are based on a broad-based index (such as the consumer price index)
- death benefit increases inherent in the policy design because of the crediting of interest or other earnings. (This appears to exempt the increasing death benefits of a type II universal life policy from classification as a material change.)
- increases in death benefits because of the premiums paid for the policy to support the level of benefits for the first 7 contract years. (This appears to exempt from material change classification any increase in death benefits necessary to keep the required relationship between the death benefit and the policy guideline cash value or guideline premiums as specified in Sec. 7702.)

A policy that was previously not classified as a MEC will be subject to the 7-pay test after a material change. If the policy then fails the test, it will be a MEC and therefore subject to LIFO taxation of policy loans, withdrawals, and terminations. The change in taxation will only be applicable for the year of the material change and subsequent years. There will not be retroactive taxation of loans or distributions in years prior to the application of the 7-pay test unless the distributions were made in anticipation of the failure or made within 2 years before such failure. In such cases the distribution will be taxed in the year it was made.

Special Rule for Death Benefit Increases over $150,000

A policy entered into prior to June 21, 1988, that experiences an increase of death benefits in excess of $150,000 on or after October 20, 1988, will be subject to the material change provisions. This means that such a policy could lose its grandfathered status if it does not pass the 7-pay test. The policy will be subject to the 7-pay test at each increase unless the death benefit increases were due to cost-of-living adjustments, to interest or earnings increases, or attributable to premiums needed to fund the lowest level of benefits during the first 7 policy years.

What increase in death benefits would be attributable to premiums needed to fund the lowest level of benefits during the first 7 policy years? If the increase in the cash value of the contract forces an increase in the death benefit in order to satisfy the definition of a life insurance contract under IRC Sec. 7702, such an increase in the death benefit is attributable to those premiums. Therefore such an increase will not cause the policy to be reclassified as a MEC.

However, the loss of grandfather status only applies to policies that require less than seven level annual premiums. If a policy required at least seven level annual premiums as of June 21, 1988, and the policyowner actually makes seven level annual premium payments, the $150,000 death benefit increase provision will not apply, and the policy will retain its grandfathered status.

Conversion Rights

Term insurance policies entered into before June 21, 1988, that are converted to cash-value policies after June 20, 1988, will be treated as if originally entered into on the date of conversion. This means that they will have to satisfy the 7-pay test at the time of conversion.

> *Example:* Angelica purchased a term life insurance policy in January 1988. On January 1, 1994, she converts her term policy to a whole life policy. Angelica's new policy is subject to the 7-pay test.

Reduction in Benefits

If there is a reduction of policy death benefits during the first 7 policy years, the 7-pay test will be applicable to the policy after the reduction. The test will be applied as if the contract had originally been issued at the reduced benefit level.

The law does allow a 90-day grace period for policy reinstatement that will prevent the conversion of the policy to MEC status if there is a reduction of benefits during the first 7 policy years because of nonpayment of premiums. In other words, a policy that lapses during the first 7 years but is reinstated within 90 days will not be reclassified as a MEC because of the temporary reduction of benefits prior to the reinstatement.

> *Example:* Bret purchased a $100,000 universal life policy on January 1, 1990. In the 5th policy year, on January 31, 1994, he negotiates a reduction in the death benefit to $70,000. Bret must now pass the 7-pay test for a $70,000 policy entered into on January 1, 1990. If the policy does not pass the test, the policy will be treated as a MEC beginning on the date the benefits were reduced, January 31, 1994.

With respect to policies entered into or materially changed on or after September 14, 1989, that insure more than one life (so-called survivorship policies), a reduction in death benefits *after* the first 7 contract years will also cause the policy to be subject to the 7-pay test as if the policy had originally been issued at the reduced benefit level. This provision was designed to plug a technical loophole in the MEC statute, which seemed to permit survivorship policies with fewer than seven annual premiums to pass the 7-pay test by taking advantage of benefit reductions after 7 years and the low probability of the death of both insureds during the first 7 policy years.

Benefit Increases Not Requiring Additional Evidence of Insurability

As previously explained, if the death benefit of a grandfathered policy increases by more than $150,000, the policy may be subjected to the material change rules and be reclassified as a MEC if it fails the 7-pay test. In addition, Congress anticipated other potential abuses with respect to grandfathered policies.

One potential abuse would be the granting of benefit increases on policies that originally did not contractually provide for such increases without additional evidence of insurability. If the insurance company provides a benefit increase on a policy after June 20, 1988, that would have required additional evidence of insurability for such an increase before June 21, 1988, the policy will be treated as if it were entered into on or after June 21, 1988. This means that the policy will be subject to the 7-pay test based on the benefit increases, regardless of whether the benefit has increased by more than $150,000. However, if the policy originally provided for benefit increases for events such as birth or marriage without additional evidence of insurability, the policy will retain its grandfathered status until the aggregate of all such benefit increases exceeds $150,000, as previously discussed.

Treatment of Premiums Returned

There is a 60-day grace period for returned premiums to keep the premiums paid under the 7-pay net level premium amount. The insurer can return excess premiums within 60 days after the end of the contract year. The returned amount will reduce the sum of premiums paid under the contract during such contract year. If any part of such payment from the insurance company is interest, it will be includible in the gross income of the recipient.

Aggregation Rules

Congress foresaw potential abuses in withdrawing funds from MECs by splitting up funds between many policies and withdrawing funds from one policy. In that manner the gain on that one policy could be withdrawn and the remainder of the withdrawals would be a nontaxable return of the policyowner's basis in the contract. To prevent this the law requires that all MECs issued by the same insurer to a policyowner during any calendar year be treated as one MEC. This forces recognition of all gain from all such policies before the policyowner is able to withdraw the investment in the contract.

> *Example:* Arnie purchased 10 single-premium life insurance policies in 1992. He paid $100,000 for each policy. On January 1, 1994, the policies have a cash value of $117,000 each.
> Arnie is now 50 years old. Arnie withdraws $50,000 of cash value from one of his policies. The aggregate increase in cash value on all of Arnie's policies is $170,000 ($17,000 x 10). Therefore the entire $50,000 withdrawal is subject to both federal income tax and the 10 percent penalty, even though the gain in the policy from which the funds were withdrawn is only $17,000.

Burial Contracts

Another provision in the new law exempts assignments or pledges of MECs with face amounts of less than $25,000 from current taxation if the assignment or pledge is for funeral services or prearranged funerals. It is important to remember that all other pledges or assignments of MECs are treated as loans from the policy. Therefore the pledge or assignment will result in both the federal income tax and the 10 percent penalty.

MEC Checklist

The following are checklists for policies that originally were not classified as MECs. They involve changes that could affect the application of a new 7-pay test.

Can a *grandfather* life insurance policy become a MEC if

	Yes	No
it remains in force with no policy	☐	☒
it has a death benefit increase of more than $150,000 after October 20, 1988	☒	☐
its death benefit increases due to a premium "dump" on or after June 21, 1988	☒	☐
it is terminated	☐	☒
it is a single life policy and is kept in force, but the death benefit is reduced after the 7th policy year	☐	☒
it is a survivorship policy and is kept in force, but the death benefit is reduced after the 7th policy year	☒	☐
it experiences death benefit increases due to interest or earnings internal to the policy	☐	☒
it has death benefit increases in order to satisfy the definition of life insurance and the premium has not increased above the level during the first 7 policy years	☐	☒
it has death benefit increases due to a cost-of-living provision linked to the consumer price index (CPI)	☐	☒
it experiences death benefit increases from exercising the guaranteed purchase provisions in the policy	☐	☒

	Yes	No
it experiences death benefit increases as a result of purchase options exercised when the insured has a newborn	☐	☒
it has an increase in benefits for which there is no policy guarantee or provision waiving evidence of insurability requirements, and such increase would normally require additional evidence of insurability	☒	☐

Can a policy entered into after June 20, 1988, that initially passes the 7-pay test be subjected to the test again if

	Yes	No
the death benefit is decreased during the first 7 policy years (or thereafter in the case of a survivorship policy)	☒	☐
the death benefit increases due to premium increases after the first 7 policy years	☒	☐
the death benefit increases due to paid-up additions from premium amounts greater than required to fund the benefit levels provided during the first 7 policy years	☒	☐
the death benefit increases due to cost-of-living adjustments tied to the CPI or some other widely accepted index	☐	☒
the death benefit must be increased to satisfy the definition of life insurance, but the premiums paid are not in excess of those required to fund the level of benefits maintained in the first 7 policy years	☐	☒

	Yes	*No*
the death benefit must be increased to satisfy the definition of life insurance because of excess interest or earnings credited inside the policy, but premiums are not in excess of those required to fund the level of benefits maintained in the first 7 policy years	☐	☒

EFFECTIVE DATE

The law does not apply to policies that were entered into prior to June 21, 1988, unless a material change occurs as previously described. Persons owning such single-premium life insurance policies should realize that they have something with tax advantages that may never be available again. Those owning policies entered into on or after June 21, 1988, will be subject to the MEC rules.

PLANNING CONSIDERATIONS

Clients who have purchased policies that are classified as MECs should not be hasty to terminate them (especially those still subject to policy surrender charges in addition to the regular income tax and 10 percent penalty tax). In summary, funds received under the policy (including policy loans or other loans secured by the modified endowment contract and dividends paid out by the policy) will be considered taxable income first. Amounts in excess of the gain in the policy will be considered tax-free recovery of cost basis. This is similar to the treatment of withdrawals of funds during the accumulation phase under a deferred annuity.

Clients owning single-premium or limited pay policies that were entered into before June 21, 1988, should be informed of the grandfathering they enjoy and that their policy loans will not be subject to LIFO-based income taxes. However, those clients must be cautioned that their special status can be lost if the policy is exchanged for a new policy that requires additional premiums or if the death benefit on the existing policy is increased in such a way that it is treated as a material change.

Owners of pre-June 21, 1988, contracts should be reminded that the law still imposes LIFO taxation on non-MEC policies that have funds withdrawn during the first 15 policy years, in association with a reduction of benefits. This is most likely to occur under type II universal life policies and single-premium policies.

Clients who purchased policies after June 20, 1988, that fail the 7-pay test should be aware that they are subject to the MEC rules. Clients should carefully consider the cost of terminating such policies before deciding what to do. At first these policies probably have relatively small gains subject to taxation and penalty, but they may face significant surrender charges. The surrender charges will decrease with policy duration, but the taxable gains will increase with duration. Each individual policy has its own pattern and trade-offs. Individual evaluations are required to determine the optimal treatment of these policies. In some cases the policyowner may be justified in terminating early and limiting taxation even though it means paying surrender charges. Some may choose to keep the policy in force but not take possession of policy cash values. All policyowners should be able to find less costly sources of funds than policy loans from a MEC.

By congressional design, single-premium policies have lost their potential for use as a strictly investment-oriented tax-deferral vehicle. However, it is important to realize and emphasize that single-premium policies can still be viable and desirable. They provide a way to pass assets to others without subjecting them to the costs, delays, and uncertainties of probate; attacks on or elections against the insured's will; or the claims of creditors. These policies also provide a way to fully prefund future debts or pledges with discounted tax-advantaged dollars. At death they are still income tax free and can be arranged to be both estate and inheritance tax free.

10

Taxation of Corporations and Shareholders

James F. Ivers III and Stephan R. Leimberg

Cheesman, Reebel, and Baily are engineers. They have developed a relatively inexpensive process for manufacturing an aircraft safety component that is in great demand for new jet airliners.

Cheesman is a sole proprietor currently engaged in producing aircraft parts. Reebel, a young man who has a postgraduate degree in business administration and an undergraduate degree in engineering, has worked for Cheesman for a number of years. He first started as an engineer and almost by accident moved into the firm's sales division. Reebel's sales efforts have been so successful that Cheesman would like to offer him an interest in a new business venture. Baily is slightly older than Cheesman and Reebel. He is a well-known and highly respected authority in the area of aircraft safety parts. He does quite a bit of consulting work for both government and private enterprise. He met Cheesman and Reebel on such a consulting project, and the three men have become good friends. Baily is quite wealthy, and he is interested in keeping both his money and his mind at work.

The three engineers have decided to form a business and have invited Bob Kress, a CPA attorney who is an expert in tax planning, to help them decide on a course of action. Kress has suggested that the best vehicle for their new business venture might be a corporation. They have asked Kress to discuss the taxation of a corporation on a detailed basis so that they could get an idea of what advantages and disadvantages corporate status entails, as well as some of the tax implications of doing business in corporate form.

Definition of a Corporation

Kress: A corporation is essentially a legal entity created under state law for the purpose of conducting a business or philanthropic activity. Federal income tax law provides its own rules for determining how such an entity should be taxed. The Internal Revenue Service as well as state and federal courts examine the presence or absence of a number of characteristics to determine if an organization is a corporation for tax purposes.[1]

These state and federal courts have varying roles. The state courts help to determine whether an organization possesses certain legal characteristics. The questions that determine the existence of such characteristics are the following:

- Is the liability of the owners (stockholders) limited?
- Could any one of those stockholders freely transfer his or her corporate interest?
- Is the management of the organization centralized?
- Does the organization have continuity of life?

Cheesman: Bob, would you go into more detail on exactly what you mean by some of those phrases?

Kress: Yes, an organization will be taxable as a corporation if it has the following elements: limited liability, transferability of interest, centralized management, and continuity of life.

An organization possesses *limited liability* if the organization's creditors cannot proceed against its individual owners personally in satisfaction of a corporate debt. This is one of the best-known reasons for choosing the corporate form.

If the formalities of corporate procedure are followed, then the corporation is really operating as a business and financial unit entirely separate from its shareholders for legal purposes. Shareholders will not be personally liable for the corporation's debts or other liabilities. As a practical matter, principal shareholders of small corporations will often be required to cosign a note or give a personal guarantee for the corporation and therefore become personally liable for loans to the corporation from banks or other lending institutions. Generally, however, the most a shareholder can lose is his or her investment in the business.[2]

Transferability of interest generally means that a member of a corporation can transfer interest in the profits, assets, and control of the business freely and without restraint. If each member, without the consent of the other members of the organization, can transfer interest to a person who is not a member, there is *free transferability of interest.* It is permissible, however, to impose reasonable restrictions on shareholders to preserve the nature of close corporate membership. These restrictions are often contained in *buy-sell* agreements and facilitate family estate planning with respect to a business interest.[3]

Centralized management exists if the operating authority is concentrated in one person or a relatively small class within the group as opposed to the sharing of management decisions commonly found in partnerships. If any person or group of persons (which does not include all of the members) has continuing, exclusive authority to make the decisions necessary to the management and daily operation of the business, there will be centralized management.

The group in which that authority is legally vested is called the board of directors. The board of directors uses its best judgment and independent discretion to determine and execute corporate policies. Although these individuals are in fact elected by the shareholders and are removable by them for cause (and possibly without cause), the directors are not agents of the shareholders. They are fiduciaries whose duties primarily run to the corporation itself.

It is the board of directors, not the shareholders, who make policy decisions with respect to the products, services, prices, and wages of the company. Likewise, even in the smallest corporation, legally speaking it is the board of directors that has the right to select, supervise, and remove officers and other personnel. For example, the board of directors, and not the shareholders, fixes compensation and decides on the installation and benefit levels of pension and profit-sharing plans, as well as other employee benefits. In short, the supervision and vigilance for the welfare of the entire corporate enterprise is vested in the hands of a very select group.[4]

Continuity of life means that death, disability, incapacity, addition of a new member, or withdrawal of an old member will not cause legal dissolution of the business. If the effect of the death of a member of the firm is the automatic death of the business, a vital element of corporate status would be lacking. A corporation is the only form of business enterprise that—theoretically at least—has the advantage of perpetual existence.[5] For example, even the death of a 100 percent stockholder would not cause the legal termination of the business. Practically speaking, however, without successor management, such a corporation will *die* as quickly as a sole proprietorship. (Some states impose limitations on corporate duration, although most jurisdictions allow a corporation to select any period of time desirable.)

Effect of Federal and State Law

Although state law determines which of these characteristics an organization possesses, it is federal law that determines which of these corporate attributes must be present for an organization to be taxed as a corporation. Generally federal courts have looked at all the facts and circumstances that affect or have been affected by the form and function of the organization in question.

The federal tax law does not limit corporate taxation merely to those organizations that are legal corporate entities under state law. For example, joint stock companies, insurance companies, associations, and even trusts may be classified as corporations because of their nature and activities. The point is that an organization's classification as a corporation does not depend on its characterization under state law or by what terms it calls itself, but rather on the number of corporate characteristics it possesses. If the corporate characteristics are such that an organization more closely resembles a corporation than a partnership or trust, for tax purposes it will be taxed as a corporation. This means that the organization will be treated as a separate taxable entity, distinct and apart from the owners (individual or corporate) of its stock. A corporation therefore has an existence separate from its shareholders. Taxwise, the result is that a corporation must compute its own income and deductions, file its own return, and pay its own tax.[6]

Types of Corporations

There are many different types of corporations. For example, there is the ecclesiastical corporation that is organized to hold property in connection with the advancement of a particular religious faith. An eleemosynary corporation is created to hold property for the benefit of a charity or benevolent society. The type of corporation you gentlemen are contemplating is a subsection of a third general type, the civil corporation. The civil corporation encompasses all corporations other than ecclesiastical or eleemosynary. The civil corporation can be political, quasi-public, or private.

Reebel: Would we be considered private?

Kress: Yes, political corporations are created by governments to manage public affairs. The Post Office Corporation is a good illustration. Sometimes companies are privately owned but exist to serve the public. Where the state maintains close control and supervision over the conduct of a corporation's business, it is considered quasi-public. An example would be a gas or electric company.

The organization you are considering would be organized for the benefit of its members, the three of you. Such a private corporation, operated for a profit, is called a "stock" company. This means that the capital of the business is divided into transferable portions known as shares that are evidenced by stock certificates. These certificates will entitle holders to participate in a distribution of profits. As you know, a certificate represents a stockholder's proportionate interest in the profits, the net assets, and the control of the corporation.

Initially your organization will probably be a private stock corporation classified as a "close" rather than a publicly traded corporation. Commonly a close corporation is one that has no shares of its stock available for purchase by or in the hands of the general public.

Someday you may want to expand the business and finance the growth with money from outside investors. In a sense, you would be *opening* the closed corporation by offering to issue shares of stock through a listing of the stock on a stock exchange or on the *over-the-counter market.*

As long as a corporation remains *close,* however, there will likely be only a few shareholders. These same people will probably also serve as directors and working officers. Therefore ownership, management, and key employees in your organization will be identical in fact—although separate for legal and tax purposes.

Disadvantages of Corporate Status

Baily: Are there reasons why we wouldn't want to operate as a corporation?

Kress: There are several disadvantages to the corporate form. Let's look at the non-tax-oriented disadvantages first. The corporate form lends itself to control of the minority by the majority. In the absence of appropriate control devices, the holder of a minority interest cannot readily cause the venture to be dissolved or force payment of dividends. For example, in the event of a shareholder's death—absent agreement on the subject—there is no easy way for the decedent's family to force a distribution of its share of corporate profits.

Another non-tax disadvantage is that a corporation has to strictly observe corporate form. This entails charter documents, bylaws, and board of directors' as well as shareholders' meetings—all a bit complicated in comparison with a sole proprietorship or partnership. Incorporating may also entail legal and accounting costs, as well as state filing fees and franchise taxes over and above those of a partnership.

Now let's consider the tax disadvantages. The basic tax disadvantage is the potential of double taxation of earnings. Since the corporation is a separate tax entity, earnings will be taxed to the corporation as earned, and then again to the shareholders if a corporate distribution to them is classified as a dividend.

Advantages of Corporate Status

However, once corporate status is attained, you'll obtain a number of benefits that may substantially outweigh the costs.

I'll discuss the non-tax advantages first. Primary among non-tax-oriented advantages is the ability to freely transfer ownership. It is relatively easy when using the corporate form to provide for a new owner's entrance and an old member's exit. Second, the corporate form affords a limited liability to its members. The corporation, and not its shareholders, is responsible for corporate obligations.

Now let's examine some of the tax-oriented advantages of corporate status. Since the three of you would be *employees* of the corporation, you would become entitled to a number of benefits that would be tax free to you and tax deductible by the corporation. For example, as an employee you would be permitted to borrow from the corporation's pension or profit-sharing plan. The corporation—as your employer—could establish a sizable group life and health insurance plan to cover you and your family, again at little or no tax cost to you. Since this would be considered an "ordinary and necessary" business expense, premium payments could be deducted by the corporation. A third benefit is that premiums on the disability income policies you each personally own and pay for with aftertax dollars could be taken over by your company, again tax free to you and tax deductible to the business.[7]

Reebel: I understand that by incorporating we would be eligible for loans from qualified deferred-compensation plans and certain other tax-favored fringe benefit arrangements.

Kress: That is correct. The Code permits the corporation to offer you—as an employee—a number of fringe benefits. Keep in mind that these benefits must be reasonable in amount and in return for services you have rendered.[8]

There are other tax-oriented factors you may find advantageous. For instance, assuming your corporation does not have to pay out substantial dividends, the overall tax result may be lower federal income taxes. It might be easiest to illustrate this point by comparing partnership with corporate tax treatment. If you formed a partnership, the three of you would be taxed on all the income you earned as partners—even if you didn't actually withdraw all your partnership earnings from the firm. However, as stockholder-employees, you would be taxed only on your salaries (assuming no dividend had to be paid). Lower total federal income tax under the corporate form may result because a new taxpaying entity, the corporation, has been created. The total tax payable depends upon how much taxable income is left inside the corporation. Let's look at the current tax rate structure for corporations.[9]

Corporate Tax Rates	
Taxable Income	**Tax Rate**
$0–$50,000	15%
$50,001–$75,000	25
$75,001–$100,000	34
$100,001–$335,000	39
$335,001–$10,000,000	34
$10,000,001–$15,000,000	35
$15,000,001–$18,333,333	38
Over $18,333,333	35

Certain corporations engaged in the business of rendering personal services are taxed at a flat rate of 35 percent. We'll discuss this further when we talk about the taxation of a corporation as a separate entity.

A corporation can generally declare and pay dividends—as well as salaries—so as to avoid *bunching* income in those years when your personal income is highest. On the other hand, if you established your business in the partnership form, you'd have little control over the receipt and taxation of income. This ability to *time* income is important, since you may be able to reduce your ultimate tax liability by allowing some income to remain in the corporation and be taxed at a 15 or 25 percent rate.

Cheesman: Is there a way to have our cake and eat it too? That is, can we get the loss flow-through so that we can deduct any corporate losses against our personal income but still get many of the benefits you just mentioned?

S Corporations

Kress: What you are referring to sounds like an *S corporation.* The Internal Revenue Code allows a closely held corporation to elect not to be taxed as a regular corporation if it meets certain requirements. Basically the result is that the corporation is not taxed as a separate entity.[10]

In other words, the corporation itself does not (with certain exceptions) pay tax.[11] Instead, corporate net income is taxed directly to its shareholders. This enables shareholders of a small, closely held corporation to obtain the tax and non-tax advantages of corporate form without its disadvantages. The S corporation election eliminates *double taxation* of a corporate income upon the payment of dividends. It also avoids the problems of a penalty on accumulated earnings as well as the personal holding company tax. Depreciation as well as corporate income and losses will be immediately passed through to the shareholders. However, some of the tax-advantaged fringe benefits that are available to employees of a regular corporation cannot be taken advantage of by shareholders of an S corporation.

All these characteristics are consistent with the underlying purpose of an S corporation, which is to promote tax neutrality when choosing the form in which to do business (for example, a sole proprietorship, partnership, or corporation). Congress felt that, to the extent tax treatment influenced the choice of business form, the result was a potential distortion of normal business practices. Therefore provisions were made in the Code to allow for S corporation treatment.

To qualify for the benefits of S corporation status, a business must have the following characteristics:

- It can have only one class of stock.
- It must have no more than 35 shareholders (a husband and wife are treated as one shareholder).
- It can have no shareholder other than an individual, an estate, or certain types of trusts. Trusts that may hold S corporation stock for an unlimited time period are voting trusts, grantor trusts, or qualified Subchapter S trusts[12] provided there is a single grantor. If less than the entire trust corpus is acquired by testamentary bequest, a grantor trust is permitted to be a shareholder for a period of 60 days following the grantor's death. But if the entire corpus of the trust is includible in the grantor's estate,

a grantor trust may be a shareholder for as long as 2 years after the grantor's death. The grantor, and not the trust, is to be treated as the shareholder. Also a trust whose sole income beneficiary receives all trust income annually can be an owner of S corporation stock. In addition, a trust that is treated as owned entirely by a person other than the grantor may own S corporation stock.

- It must be a domestic corporation—that is, incorporated in the United States.
- It cannot have any subsidiaries or parent corporation.
- No shareholder can be a nonresident alien.[13]

An S corporation elects to avoid paying corporate tax on its income. The result is that the shareholders are taxed on the taxable income of the corporation in proportion to their shareholdings. If the corporation has a loss, it can be deducted directly by the shareholders. As I have already noted, using this type of election, the corporation and its shareholders are taxed in most (but not all) respects in a manner similar to the way they would be taxed if they were operating as a partnership.

The S corporation election is used in a number of situations. For example, if you expected high initial losses in your first year or two of business operations, you would want to *pass through* the corporation's losses since you are all in high individual income tax brackets, so that you could use them against your own income tax liability.[14]

An S corporation election might also be indicated where business owners want to take advantage of limited liability but do not want to incur a double taxation when income earned and taxed by the corporation is later distributed to its shareholders.

An S corporation election may also be indicated when shareholders intend to withdraw substantially all corporate earnings and (1) not all stockholders are employees who could justify their shares as salary payments, (2) the amount of earnings is so great that any attempt to pay them out as salaries would result in unreasonably high salaries, or (3) the corporation has taxable income that would be taxed at a corporate rate higher than the shareholders' individual marginal rates without an S election. The S corporation election avoids the double tax that occurs to both a corporation and its shareholders when an actual or constructive dividend is paid out of earnings. Note, however, that the top individual rate of 39.6 percent exceeds the current top corporate rate of 39 percent.

By an irrevocable and unqualified gift of shares of stock, a taxpayer can arrange to *split income* with another family member. Thus it is possible to transfer income to lower-bracket donees. By getting stock into the hands of various family members, it is possible to shift income to other taxpayers despite the fact that the income may be used to satisfy support or other family obligations that the donor would otherwise have to pay with aftertax dollars.

In fact, you could even use the S corporation election to allow the corporation to continue income payments to you at retirement (or to your widow should you predecease her) without double tax consequences. You know that the IRS questions high salaries to older stockholder-employees, often claiming that part of the pay is really a nondeductible, fully taxable dividend in disguise. The election generally avoids this question since payments to shareholders are not taxed as dividends. Thus where a shareholder is inactive, less able to contribute time or services, or where he or she needs income upon retirement but does not want to create a double tax, the S corporation election may be the answer.

Baily: How long is the S corporation election effective?

Kress: Once made, an S election is effective indefinitely. However, the election can be terminated in any of the following ways.

First, the corporation can elect to revoke the election with the consent of the shareholders who own more than 50 percent of the stock.

Second, the election terminates if the corporation no longer qualifies as a "small business corporation"—that is, if it has more than 35 shareholders, or a nonresident alien acquires stock, or if an entity other than permitted shareholders acquires stock. Also the issuance of a second class of stock would terminate the election.

Third, if more than 25 percent of the S corporation's gross receipts for 3 successive tax years is from certain types of passive income and the corporation has accumulated earnings and profits from its days prior to the S election, the election will be terminated.[15]

The revocation can be elected on or before the 15th day of the third month of the present taxable year and will be effective for that entire taxable year, unless the revocation specifically requests a revocation date in the future. If so, the revocation will be effective on the date selected. If no future date of revocation is specified but the revocation election is filed after the permissible period, the revocation is effective at the beginning of the following taxable year. As with prior law, voluntary revocations result in an inability to reelect the S status for 5 years without obtaining IRS consent to the reelection. The IRS can, in appropriate circumstances, waive the 5-year waiting period and permit the corporation to make a new election effective for the following taxable year.

Let's get back to our discussion of regular corporations. Technically, there are no clearly discernible stages of a corporation's life. However, for illustrative purposes, let's think of the tax life of your proposed corporation in terms of the following four stages: (1) birth, (2) adolescence, (3) maturity, and (4) death.

Formation of a Corporation

Kress: All three of you have something to contribute to the corporation. In return you will want to participate in the control and profits of the business while it is running or in a distribution of the assets of your business if the corporation's life ends. In other words, you will expect *shares* of the corporation. For discussion purposes, let's assume Cheesman will contribute his business (his sole proprietorship). Baily will contribute cash or securities. Reebel wants to contribute his services and a small amount of cash in return for his stock.

Assuming this is the case, here is what might happen: if Baily decides that his contribution to the capital of the corporation will be cash, the stock he receives will normally have a value at the time of the exchange equal to the cash. For example, if he transfers $10,000 of cash to the corporation, he will ordinarily receive back stock with a fair market value of $10,000. Since the value of the stock he receives is no more or less than the value of the cash he transfers to the corporation, he realizes neither a gain nor a loss. If he later sells his stock, the cash he paid will determine the basis of his stock. If he realizes $21,000 on the sale of the stock, his gain would be $11,000, the difference between his basis for the stock ($10,000) and the amount he realizes on the sale ($21,000).[16]

Reebel: Is it correct to assume that, as long as the value of the cash and/or property we transfer to the corporation is equal to the value of the stock we get, we will have neither gain nor loss?

Kress: Not exactly. The general rule is that when property is exchanged for stock in a corporation, there is a *sale or exchange*. In the absence of any other provisions in the Code, you would have a recognized gain or loss. The amount of gain or loss would be measured by the difference between the amount you realize in the transaction (the value of stock you get) and the adjusted basis (the cost) of the property transferred to the corporation. Therefore, if you transferred mutual funds that had a present fair market value of $100,000 in exchange for $100,000 of the newly formed corporation's stock, you might still have a taxable gain. For example, if you paid only $10,000 for the mutual funds (now worth $100,000) and you exchanged the mutual funds for stock, there would be a taxable gain of $90,000. This same general principle applies if Cheesman was to exchange his appreciated business for cash—he would have a gain. The same result could occur when you transferred appreciated property to the corporation in exchange for its stock.[17]

Reebel: I guess that rules out Cheesman putting in his sole proprietorship and also Baily transferring his appreciated securities into a new corporation.

Kress: Not really—what we have just discussed is the general rule. But, like most provisions of the Code, there is an exception to the general rule. The exception was designed to encourage the formation of new corporations. It enables a taxpayer to transfer appreciated property or even a going business into a new corporation without the transferor recognizing income on the appreciation at the very time when his or her other expenses—the expenses involved in the organization and operation of the corporation—are the highest. The exception provides that even if the transferor *realizes* a gain when appreciated property is transferred to his or her new corporation, gain does not have to be *recognized* for tax purposes.[18]

Nonrecognition Provision for Transfer to a Corporation Controlled by Transferor(s)

This exception is conditioned on meeting some basic requirements. It essentially states that where a person or persons transfer property to a corporation (1) solely in exchange for the corporation's own stock, and (2) the transferor(s) control the corporation immediately after the transfer, no gain will be recognized on the appreciated property or securities contributed to the new corporation.

The philosophy here is similar to the theory making a like-kind exchange tax free. The transferor who receives stock in exchange for property has really maintained interest in the original property. It has merely changed form. The new form continues his or her interest in the original property, though it now has the physical identity of *stock*. This *continuity-of-interest* concept is the key to nonrecognition of the gain on the appreciated property transferred.

For example, suppose Cheesman, who is now operating as a sole proprietor, decides to transfer his going business to the new corporation. If his basis for the sole proprietorship is $10,000 and the fair market value of his business is $50,000 at the time he transfers it to the new corporation, he would probably receive $50,000 worth of stock. Under the general rule for taxing sales and exchanges, he would recognize a $40,000 gain. However, the nonrecognition provision provides that since he got back only stock and through that stock controlled the corporation (just as he previously controlled his sole proprietorship), what has happened in really only the substitution of stock certificates for his former physical possession of the property. In other words, he now owns stock that is evidence of ownership in the same property owned before. His interest has changed merely in form, not in substance.

This rule is logical since to recognize gain there must be a taxable event that usually occurs in the form of a sale, or exchange, or other disposition of property. Although technically there may be a sale (a transfer of property in return for money or a promise to pay money) or exchange (a transfer of property in return for other property or services), there has been no exchange in substance. Cheesman, in our example, hasn't disposed of his property. He has merely received certificates that evidence that he changed the form (and not substance) of his ownership in the original property. This would apply no matter how many people transfer property to the corporation. As long as it was done collectively, if the taxpayers transferring property to the corporation still have both (1) control and (2) interest in the property they originally owned, they would not have to recognize any gain on receipt of the new corporation's stock. Thus Cheesman would not have to recognize the $40,000 gain until and unless he later sells his stock.

Requirements for Nonrecognition

There are three formal requirements that must be satisfied to obtain an exception to the general rule so that there will be no recognition of a gain. Perhaps this chart will help.

Nonrecognition Provision		

If the transfer of property is
  a. solely in exchange for the corporation's own stock and
  b. transferor(s) control the corporation immediately after
     the transfer, then no gain (or loss) is recognized.		

Money or Other Property Received to Boot		

Receives
  Stock
  Cash
	$30,000
	$20,000	

Transfers
  Property (Basis)
  Gain
  Reportable*
		$50,000
		
		$10,000
		$40,000
		$20,000

*Gain ($40,000) is recognized to extent of *boot* ($20,000).		

First, there must be one or more persons transferring property (which may include cash) to the newly formed corporation. The example we have just discussed meets the *transfer-of-property* requirement, since we assumed Cheesman transferred his business to the corporation.

Second, the transfer must be *solely in exchange* for stock in such a corporation. Since all Cheesman received from the corporation was the stock of the new corporation, the example above meets this requirement. If, however, Cheesman had received stock plus *other property* (such as cash or corporate notes) his transfer would not have met this requirement. If he had received stock (which does qualify) plus that other property *to boot* (other property or cash which does not qualify), he would have had to recognize part of his gain. Generally to the extent of this *boot* received, or to the extent of the gain on his transaction (whichever is less), the transferor of appreciated property will have to recognize income. For example, in the situation above, if Cheesman had received $30,000 worth of stock plus $20,000 of cash, he would have received $20,000 worth of boot. He would have to recognize income to the extent of the cash he received ($20,000), since the figure is the lower of (a) $20,000 boot or (b) the $40,000 gain realized ($50,000 amount realized minus $10,000 basis for the sole proprietorship transferred).[19]

The third requirement for nonrecognition is that the transferors (the person or persons transferring cash and/or property to the corporation in return for stock of the corporation) must be "in control immediately after" the exchange. This requirement also makes sense. For nonrecognition to follow, the incorporation must be merely a change in the physical form of ownership—that is, an exchange of cash and/or property in return for stock.

If the original transferors no longer own their original property (where there has been a drastic shift in the proportion of ownership interest and control), the transaction takes on the effect of a sale or exchange and, as such, will be taxable. Control is defined as ownership of stock possessing at least 80 percent of the combined voting power, plus at least 80 percent of the total number of shares of the new corporation. This 80 percent test of control must be met for tax purposes even though, from a legal standpoint, a shareholder could actually control a corporation with as little as a 51 percent interest.

If the three tests are met (that is, if any one of you or even all three of you transfer property to a corporation, if the transfer is solely in exchange for the stock of the new corporation, and if you as transferors are in control immediately after the exchange), the following will result.

First, no gain will have to be recognized on the exchange either by the transferor(s) or by the corporation. Second, the corporation takes the transferor's basis for the property contributed. If Cheesman's basis for the property he transfers to the corporation was $10,000 and the corporation later sells that same property, its basis for tax purposes would be $10,000. Thus if it sold the property for $30,000, its gain would be the difference, or $20,000. Third, the stockholder who receives stock from the corporation takes a substituted basis—that is, for tax purposes his or her basis for the stock acquired from the corporation is typically the same as the stockholder's basis for the property he or she transferred.

If a stockholder receives boot, he or she must (1) decrease the stock's basis to the extent of the fair market value of any boot property as well as any cash received, but (2) his or her basis can be increased by the amount of any gain that must be recognized. If Cheesman, for example, received $40,000 worth of stock plus $20,000 in cash boot, he would report the $20,000 of cash as income. Therefore Cheesman must (1) decrease the basis of his stock by $20,000 since this is the amount of the boot he received; then (2) he may increase his basis by the amount of any gain that he must recognize. Since he recognizes $20,000 of income in this particular situation, the net result of the boot transaction is a $10,000 basis. Basis is first decreased by the amount of boot received but then increased by the amount of boot that was taxable. In this case it resulted in a *washout* so that Cheesman's basis remains at $10,000.

The basis to the corporation of the property received would be the transferor's basis ($10,000), plus the amount of gain the transferor had to recognize because of the boot he or she received ($20,000). Suppose the corporation later sold the property it received. If the amount the corporation realized on the sale of the property was $40,000, its gain would be only $10,000 ($40,000 amount realized less $30,000 adjusted basis [$10,000 original basis, plus $20,000 increase in basis because of the recognition of income by the transferor]). No gain or loss is recognized by a corporation for the receipt of cash or property in exchange for stock of the corporation.

Organizational Expenditures

Baily: Are the expenses of forming a corporation currently deductible in determining corporate taxable income?

Kress: The costs of creating a corporation ordinarily constitute capital expenditures. This means that those costs may be amortized (that is, taken as equal annual deductions against income of the corporation), since in a sense they create an *asset* that will be exhausted over the lifetime of the corporation.

There are a number of such expenses created in the organization of the corporation. For example, there are state filing fees and legal expenses in obtaining the charter, costs for accounting services incident to the organization, and fees paid for drafting the corporation charter and bylaws as well as for the terms of the original stock certificates. A corporation can elect to recover the cost of these organizational expenditures through amortization deductions. In other words, the corporation can elect to deduct these costs in even amounts over a period of 5 years or longer beginning with the month in which the corporation begins business. In most cases this would be after the charter is issued.[20]

Other Methods of Financing

One of the key advantages of business in the corporate form is that many different types of ownership interests in corporations can be created. We have just discussed the general definition of stock. This includes common stock, preferred stock, convertible securities, warrants, and options. The interests of any particular investor can be met by creating a security that fits his or her special needs and desires. This factor facilitates the acquisition of capital. Suppose the corporation issued bonds to acquire working capital as well as capital for long-term planning. As you know, a bond is a written obligation to repay a definite sum of money on a definite date, usually at least 10 and more often 20 or more years, from the date the bond was issued.

Bonds are a favored means of raising corporate capital. One reason for this is that a corporation will obtain a deduction for the interest paid on the indebtedness. By contrast, no deduction is allowed for dividends paid on either preferred or common stock. As long as a corporation can earn money at a higher rate (with the cash raised by issuing the bond) than it costs the corporation (in interest necessary to *service the debt),* it usually makes sense for the corporation to borrow money. This is known as "leverage."

Of course, issuance of the bonds themselves would create no tax liability to either the corporation or the bondholder. This is because the corporation has merely borrowed money and agreed to return it. Conversely, the bondholders have merely loaned money. When the bond *matures,* the principal becomes payable and the bondholders are entitled to a tax-free return of their capital investment. In contrast, when a corporation makes payments to its shareholders with respect to their stock, the general rule is that the payment will be taxed as a dividend.

Any money bondholders receive in the form of interest will be taxable as ordinary income, while any money they receive at the maturity of their bonds in excess of their capital investment may be taxed as capital gain. This occurs when bonds are purchased at a discount but are paid off at face value. (When bonds are issued at a discount by the issuing corporation, a bondholder generally must include a ratable portion of the discount in income each year as the bond matures. For example, if a bond with a par value of $1,000 was issued for $800 and is payable in 10 years, the $200 discount would be included in the taxpayer's income at the rate of $20 a year.)

Another reason bonds are favored over stock is that the accumulation of earnings and profits within the corporation to pay debt obligations can be justified more readily than accumulating earnings to redeem stock. This helps avoid an additional tax on an unreasonable accumulation of earnings.

Reebel: Is there any reason stockholders couldn't lend money to the corporation in return for bonds?

Kress: No, it is quite common for a shareholder to forgo an equity (stock) interest with regard to some of his or her contribution in return for the greater security of a loan. As you know, the bond promises to pay a specified sum of money by a specified date. This date is usually at least 10 years from the date of issue. Of course, bonds generally pay a fixed rate of interest each year until that specified date. Typically, in the event the corporation fails financially, bondholders have preferred rights to corporate assets. Since the interest paid on corporate indebtedness is deductible, the aftertax cost of raising capital through long-term corporate debt is substantially reduced.

However, some shareholders attempt to overdo it—they contribute almost no equity investment and characterize the major portion of their contribution as debt owed to them by the corporation. This is known as "thin capitalization," since the equity investment is *thin* in relation to the debt, but the *debt* is really disguised stock.

Reebel: What is the effect of thin capitalization?

Kress: Once the form of the debt is disregarded by the IRS and the substance is treated appropriately, corporate deductions for *interest* payments to shareholders are disallowed. Second, receipt of interest payments by shareholder-creditors are reclassified and treated as dividends. Third, when the corporation pays off its debt to the shareholders, that payment is taxed as a dividend. This means that instead of treating the amount received as a tax-free repayment of a debt, the shareholder-creditor must report the entire distribution as ordinary income. Finally, money that the corporation purportedly was accumulating to pay off the debt is now subject to the accumulated-earnings tax, which we'll discuss in a few moments. Also a debt that is reclassified as stock could cause a termination of an S election since an S corporation is allowed to have only one class of stock.

Baily: How do the courts distinguish between debt and equity?

Kress: The courts usually examine a number of factors such as, Was there an intention by shareholders to enforce payment of the debt? Was there collateral for the debt? Was there a debt instrument (note), and did it give the shareholders management or voting rights (like stock)? What was the ratio of debt to equity? A rule of thumb is that if the amount of debt exceeds shareholders' equity by more than four to one, the corporation is thinly capitalized. Basically the court would examine all the factors relevant to determine if a "loan" by shareholders was in reality more like an ownership interest (stock) than a debtor-creditor relationship.[21]

Keep in mind that while bonds are a tax-favored means of obtaining corporate funds, frequently a corporation does not want to become obligated to make fixed payments for interest and debt amortization. To avoid a cash-flow problem, therefore, corporations often finance long-term operations or investments with common stock, which entails no obligation to pay dividends, or preferred stock on which dividend payments can frequently be avoided. Furthermore, stocks are used in preference to bonds because, unlike bonds, stocks never *mature*—there is no requirement that a corporation pay off either preferred or common stock.

Cheesman: Assuming we've properly capitalized the corporation, how is its income actually taxed?

Taxation as a Separate Entity

Kress: A corporation is taxed as an entity separate from its shareholders. The rates are 15 percent of the first $50,000 of taxable income, 25 percent of the next $25,000, 34 percent on amounts of taxable income between $75,001 and $100,000, 39 percent on amounts between $100,001 and $335,000, 34 percent on amounts between $335,001 and $10 million, 35 percent on amounts from $10 million to $15 million, 38 percent on amounts from $15 million to $18,333,333, and 35 percent on amounts over $18,333,333. Thus if your corporation (let's call it the Bradwell Corporation) has $60,000 of taxable income, its tax will be $10,000 (15 percent of $50,000, plus 25 percent of the $10,000 excess above $50,000).[22]

However, under current law the taxable income of a "qualified personal service corporation" will be taxed at a flat rate of 35 percent. A qualified personal service corporation for this purpose is one in which (1) substantially all the activities involve the performance of services in the fields of health, law, engineering, architecture, accounting, actuarial science, performing arts, or consulting, and (2) substantially all the stock (95 percent or more) is held by employees or retired employees or by their estates.

Since the Bradwell Corporation will be engaged in a manufacturing business, the flat rate of 35 percent will not apply. However, should the Bradwell Corporation become a consulting business in the future, the flat tax rate would apply since all three shareholders will be working for the business. This, of course, is only the federal income tax. Corporations, like individuals, are liable for a number of other state and local taxes as well. Bradwell Corporation would report its federal income tax on IRS Form 1120.

Graphically, Bradwell Corporation's return might look like the illustration on the following page.

Computation of Taxable Income

Gross income would include such items as profit from sales and receipts from services. It would also include gains on sales or exchanges, income from rent, royalties, interest, and dividends.

A corporation is entitled to two types of deductions—ordinary deductions and special deductions. Ordinary deductions would include compensation of officers and salaries, bonuses, rent payments, charitable contributions, repair expenses, interest paid on indebtedness, casualty losses, deductions for depreciation and amortization of research and experimental costs, advertising, and corporate contributions to pension and profit-sharing plans. A corporation would also receive a carryover deduction for a net operating loss.

Several deductions are classified as "special." One of these items is known as a "dividends-received" deduction. This deduction reduces gross income by 70 percent of dividends received from certain other corporations. In other words, a corporation will pay tax on only 30 percent of the amount of such dividends. The deduction may be either 80 percent or 100 percent of dividends received, rather than 70 percent, if the receiving corporation owns specified percentages of the stock of the paying corporation.[23]

Taxable income is what is left after taking ordinary and special deductions. It is the amount to which the corporate income tax rates are applied. Certain credits are then directly applied against this tax, such as corporate overpayments of tax in previous years, payments for estimated taxes (paid on a quarterly basis), credit on certain foreign taxes paid, and investment credit.

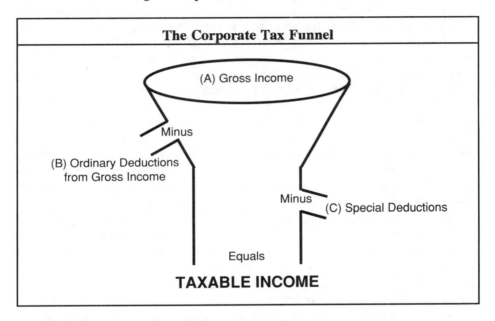

The Corporate Tax Funnel

(A) Gross Income

Minus

(B) Ordinary Deductions from Gross Income

Minus (C) Special Deductions

Equals

TAXABLE INCOME

Kress: Let me go into more detail on some of those items.

Deductions for Salaries

The first item we discussed under the category of "ordinary deductions" was salaries. Bradwell Corporation would be entitled to a deduction for salaries or any other compensation for personal services, but only if the services were actually rendered and the amount paid as compensation for those services was considered *reasonable.* Reasonable means only the amount that would ordinarily be paid for similar services by corporations like Bradwell under similar circumstances.

This reasonableness test is imposed most frequently on closely held corporations because of the large degree of coincidence of executive and shareholder interest. It is designed to prevent the shareholders of Bradwell from draining out corporate profits in the disguise of tax-deductible salaries. Corporate profits are usually paid out in the form of dividends that are taxable to the shareholders but are nondeductible by the corporation. The portion of the salary considered unreasonable is usually classified as a disguised dividend, and to that extent the corporation's deduction is disallowed. However, even though that amount may not be deducted by the corporation, it is still taxable as ordinary income to the shareholder-recipient.[24]

Reasonableness is a question of determining the amount that would ordinarily be paid for like services by like enterprises under like circumstances. Generally, where an executive employee does not own or have options to purchase stock, arm's-length bargaining as to the amount of salary is assumed. One element that could be considered in determining reasonableness is the fact that a given individual was not adequately compensated in prior years. Thus if high compensation in the current year can be attributed to services rendered in prior years, the total current salary might be considered reasonable.

However, the amount of cash compensation is not the only relevant factor. Corporate contributions to pension and profit-sharing plans are considered business expenses and are allowed as deductions as long as the total amount of all forms of compensation paid on behalf of an individual does not exceed a reasonable total. Some of the other indirect forms of compensation may be premiums for life insurance, hospitalization, medical care, and salary continuation plans.

Costs of these plans, although deductible by the corporation, often do not result in taxable income to the individual. Since the corporation is a separate and distinct tax entity, and since the three of you would be considered salaried employees, you would be eligible for these forms of indirect compensation. This is true even though you would be not only employees, but also officers, directors, and shareholders of the corporation.

With respect to reasonable payments to executives or key employees, you should be aware of a concept called *excess golden parachute payments*. These are payments to executives or key employees (1) that are contingent upon a change or threatened change of ownership or control of a corporation, and (2) that have a present value equal to or in excess of three times the individual's average annual compensation for the 5 preceding years. These payments are not deductible by the corporation, and they subject the individual to an excise tax of 20 percent of the excess payment in addition to the regular income tax.

In addition, if compensation paid to an executive fits the definition of "excessive employee remuneration," the compensation will not be deductible by the employer.

Cheesman: What is "excessive employee remuneration"?

Kress: First, the compensation must be paid by a publicly held corporation to fall within the rule. Second, the definition applies generally to compensation of over $1 million per year paid to one employee.

Compensation for purposes of this definition does *not* include commissions, contributions to qualified plans, and tax-free fringe benefits. It also does not include any compensation that is "performance based." In order to be treated as performance based, the compensation must be payable solely on account of the attainment of one or more performance goals determined by a compensation committee of the corporation's board of directors. Such a committee must be comprised solely of two or more outside directors. Also, in order to be treated as performance based, the compensation must be both disclosed to the corporation's shareholders and approved by a shareholder vote.

The $1 million limitation applies only to the chief executive officer of the company and its four highest compensated officers for the taxable year. Therefore it will apply only to a maximum of five employees in any given corporation. If the corporation has made so-called excess golden parachute payments that are nondeductible under IRC Sec. 280(G), such payments will reduce the $1 million annual cap.

Charitable Deduction

It is generally felt that corporations owe some type of obligation to the communities in which they exist. Consequently the corporate statutes of most states permit corporations to make charitable contributions. The Internal Revenue Code permits a charitable deduction for contributions by a corporation. However, the deduction is limited to a maximum of 10 percent of the corporation's taxable income. (Certain adjustments are made to taxable income before the 10 percent maximum deduction is computed. For example, taxable income for this purpose is computed without regard to the deduction for charitable contributions in order to avoid a circular calculation.) If the corporation should make a contribution in excess of 10 percent of its adjusted taxable income, it can carry the deduction forward for up to 5 years and use that carryforward to reduce its future taxable income. For example, if taxable income was $100,000, and the corporation made a charitable deduction of $100,000, it would get a $10,000 ordinary deduction it could use in the current year. The balance could be carried over and applied against future years' income.[25]

Net Operating Loss

Suppose Bradwell Corporation didn't do as well as originally planned. In fact, suppose the expenses of operating the business exceeded the corporation's income. Because a corporation is treated as a separate tax entity, losses will not be allowed to pass through to Bradwell's shareholders. Unlike the case in a partnership or S corporation, a normal corporation's shareholders will not be able to use a loss to offset personal income. The loss may only be used by the corporation itself. Bradwell could use this net operating loss to reduce income in certain other tax years. In other words, if the corporation has more operating expenses than it has income, it could carry the loss as a deduction to certain other tax years. The loss would then reduce tax liability for the year to which it is carried. Unlike charitable deductions where the corporation is only allowed to carry a deduction forward, in the case of a net operating loss, the corporation can *carry back* the loss and then also carry it forward.

The corporation can carry the loss back 3 years and carry it forward 15 years. The effect of such provision is to enable a corporation to average operating gain or loss over a continuous 19-year period. The process works like this: First, the corporation carries back its loss just as if that loss had actually been incurred 3 years before the year in which the loss was actually sustained. Appropriate adjustments are made on that year's tax return. Then any unused loss is carried back to the second year preceding the actual year when the loss is sustained. Then it is carried back one year. If there is any excess loss not applied to back years, the remaining net operating loss is carried forward over the next 15 years.

A corporation may elect not to utilize the carryback period, even though this does not extend the carryforward period. A corporate taxpayer may waive the carryback period when it was in an unusually low bracket or when it was already shielded by tax credits that could not be carried to later years.

The purpose of the carryback or carryforward of operating losses is to enable the corporate taxpayer to stabilize business income. If there were no provisions for carrying operating losses backward or forward, the entire gain from successful years would be taxed, but in loss years only a portion of the loss could be utilized. A loss in a given year that exceeded earnings for that year would be useless.

Capital Gains and Losses

Often a corporation will sell or exchange capital assets. If Bradwell sells a capital asset at a loss, then, unlike an individual, it may not apply any portion of that loss against ordinary income. A corporation can use capital losses only as an offset against capital gains. Corporations are permitted to carry an unused net capital loss back 3 years and then, if further loss still remains, carry the excess over to the 5 succeeding years. Note that the loss still cannot be used to reduce ordinary income. Corporate capital losses must be utilized only to offset capital gains. Such losses must first be applied to the earliest of the years involved (3 back—5 forward), then to the next year, and so on until the losses are exhausted.[26]

Cheesman: What if the sale resulted in a gain?

Kress: A corporation must include its full capital gain in income. However, there is an alternative method of taxation that may apply to a corporation's capital gains in some cases. The alternative method provides for a flat rate of 35 percent instead of the regular corporate tax rates. The alternative tax applies only if the applicable regular tax rate is higher than 35 percent (compared without regard to the 38 percent bracket). If the corporation's taxable income (including the capital gain) does not exceed $100,000, the regular rates must be used for capital gains. For corporations with taxable income in excess of $100,000, the determination is more complex and subject to a technical ambiguity in the Code. The following is a comparison assuming that the corporation has $75,000 of taxable income this year, which includes $5,000 of net long-term capital gain:

Corporation Has $75,000 of Taxable Income			
Regular Tax Computation		Alternative Tax Computation	
(1) 15% of $50,000 of taxable income	$7,500	(1) Taxable income	$75,000
(2) 25% of taxable income between $50,001 and $75,000	$6,250	(2) Less—$5,000 net long-term capital gain	$ 5,000
			$70,000
		(3) Tax on $70,000 at regular rates	$12,500
		(4) 35% of $5,000 capital gain	$ 1,750
Regular tax	$13,750	Alternative tax	$14,250

Note: The alternative method of taxation would not be used in this example because it is more than the regular tax.

Deduction for Dividends Received from Certain Corporations

I mentioned before that a corporation may be entitled to certain *special* deductions. The most common of the special deductions is the deduction for dividends received from certain corporations. For example, Bradwell Corporation might purchase stock in other corporations, such as AT&T or General Motors, as an investment. Perhaps Baily will transfer stock of other corporations to Bradwell Corporation as part of his original contribution of capital in return for Bradwell's stock. Bradwell would be allowed a special deduction for a percentage of dividends received during its tax year from stock it holds in certain other corporations. Specifically, it may deduct (subject to certain limitations) 70 percent of the dividends it receives.

These dividends must be distributions from the earnings and profits of taxable domestic corporations. Since dividends on deposit or withdrawal accounts in domestic building and loan associations or mutual savings banks are not really dividends at all, they are treated as interest and do not qualify for this deduction.

Likewise, Bradwell cannot deduct 70 percent of the dividends received from many tax-exempt corporations, because the deduction for dividends received is intended to prevent triple taxation of corporate income. Since tax-exempt corporations and many foreign corporations are either not taxed at all or not taxed at full corporate rates, to allow a *dividends-received* deduction for dividends received from these corporations would be to favor them rather than to treat them equitably.[27]

The amount of the dividends-received deduction can vary depending on how much stock in the paying corporation is owned by the receiving corporation. The dividends-received deduction is 70 percent if the receiving corporation owns less than 20 percent of the paying corporation. If the receiving corporation owns 20 percent or more but less than 80 percent of the paying corporation, the dividends-received deduction is 80 percent. Different rules apply if the corporation receiving the dividends owns 80 percent or more of the corporation paying the dividends. If certain conditions are met, the dividends-received deduction is 100 percent.

There is a reduction in the dividends-received deduction when the corporation owns a portfolio of stock acquired by incurring debt. The theory is that the benefit of the dividends-received deduction should be neutralized, since the corporation obtained the added benefit of a deduction for interest on the debt incurred to purchase stock.

The dividends-received deduction is not available to S corporations.

The Accumulated-Earnings Tax

Assuming that Bradwell Corporation is as successful as the three of you have been individually, in a few years the corporation will reach its maturity stage. As the corporation begins to be profitable, it will need money to grow and expand, just as it needed capital at its formation. One of the easiest ways of financing growth is by accumulating earnings and plowing them back into the corporation to purchase new machinery, buildings, and other necessary capital assets. These *plow-back* earnings and profits begin to add up very quickly. You may want to use your business as a vehicle for accumulating money. You can do that merely by having the corporation retain earnings rather than make distributions to shareholders in the form of nondeductible dividends. If Bradwell Corporation allows earnings to accumulate in order to fund current or anticipated needs or projects that the corporation has planned, there is no problem. However, once earnings are allowed to accumulate beyond the reasonable needs of the business, those earnings may be subject to an additional tax.[28]

The accumulated-earnings tax is a tax imposed on every corporation that is formed or used for the purpose of avoiding personal income tax with respect to its shareholders by permitting earnings and profits to accumulate instead of being distributed. The purpose of the tax is to discourage the use of a corporation as an accumulation vehicle to shelter its individual stockholders from taxation resulting from dividend distributions. Without such a tax on improper accumulations, stockholders could arrange to have dividends paid in years when their incomes were low, or they could indefinitely accumulate earnings and profits inside the corporation until the corporation was liquidated. Accumulations of $250,000 or less will automatically be considered to be for the reasonable needs of the business. Accumulations of $150,000 or less will be considered to be for the reasonable needs of the business in the case of professional service corporations.[29] However, if Bradwell is profitable and begins to accumulate amounts in excess of $250,000, it should be prepared to show a bona fide business reason for not distributing these earnings in the form of dividends.

As I mentioned, the purpose of this tax is to discourage the corporation from retaining profits in the absence of legitimate business motives. If earnings could remain in the corporation indefinitely, then its stockholders might never have to pay personal income tax on corporate earnings and profits. As a regulatory device, the accumulated-earnings tax was designed to force the distribution of retained earnings at the point where they no longer serve a legitimate business purpose.

The accumulated-earnings tax is designed to tax only earnings retained beyond the reasonable needs of the business. The question then becomes, What reasonable needs would Bradwell Corporation have for accumulating profits? The regulation states that working capital needs and capital for building expansion or for the replacement of plant or equipment are among the needs that would allow Bradwell to properly accumulate earnings. In addition to these needs, a sinking fund to retire corporate bonds at maturity has often been found to be a reasonable need to accumulate cash. In other cases, funds set aside to acquire minority interests or quarreling stockholders' interests were also deemed to be retained for reasonable business needs.[30]

Baily: Our CLU suggested we purchase cash value key person insurance. Would accumulated earnings in the form of cash values be a reasonable business need?

Kress: That depends on whether or not the insurance answers a valid corporate business need. There must also be a close correlation between the type of policy and amount of death benefit and the alleged corporate need. Generally, hedging against the loss of a key employee's service because of unexpected death is considered to be a reasonable business need.

Key person life insurance is insurance owned by the corporation insuring the life of a key employee. The purpose of such a policy is to provide a fund at the employee's death that will compensate the corporation for the financial loss resulting from the unavailability of the employee to render services to the corporation. Often key person insurance death proceeds are also used to help in finding and compensating a suitable replacement. Therefore the purchase of life insurance as well as the earnings used to pay policy premiums should not be, per se, subject to the penalty tax.[31]

In one case enough insurance to generate $1.5 million worth of life insurance proceeds was considered reasonable. The point is that it is not the amount but the purpose of the accumulation that is important.

The same question often arises as to the effect of a split-dollar plan. If a corporation attempts to prevent taxation of income to shareholders by accumulating its earnings rather than distributing them, the existence or nonexistence of a split-dollar policy will not, by itself, deter the imposition of the tax penalty provided by the law. Conversely, the existence of a split-dollar policy will not, per se, incur the accumulations tax penalty if the corporation is not, in fact, accumulating earnings beyond the reasonable needs of the business. It is important to remember that this section of the Code exists to deter tax evasion and not to prevent a business from operating in a normal businesslike manner. The same principle applies in cases where the corporation has obligated itself to make preretirement death benefits to a key executive under a deferred-compensation agreement. An accumulation of corporate earnings to meet obligations under such an agreement is generally considered a reasonable business need (just as the funds accumulated to retire an outstanding corporate bond would be considered reasonable).[32]

This question also often arises when accumulated earnings are used to provide surplus cash for the redemption of stock. In this case, if the redemption is to be utilized to shift partial or complete control to the remaining shareholders without depleting their personal funds (for example, if by shareholder agreement the corporation will retire shares on the death of a shareholder), it is doubtful that accumulations to reach this result would be found to be a reasonable need. However, if a business purpose can be found, such as an accumulation to purchase the shares of the dissenting minority, then the accumulation will be found to be reasonable. The primary purpose must be a corporate, rather than an individual, benefit from the stock redemption.[33]

Reebel: What is the maximum we could reasonably accumulate?

Kress: The critical factor is not the size of the accumulated earnings and profits but rather the reasonableness and nature of that surplus. For this reason, part of the surplus may be justifiably earmarked in the form of reserves for specific business needs.

Keep in mind that for the tax to be imposed it is not necessary that tax avoidance be the primary reason for the accumulation. As long as it is even one of the purposes for retention of earnings, the tax could be levied.

Most corporations will have little trouble in proving a reasonable business need for most of the earnings they retain. However, a corporation must be prepared to create and preserve adequate records to show that it had a specific plan to use the assets accumulated.

Among the evidence that could be used to support the corporation's case might be the fact that the business in question needs large amounts of cash for operating purposes at certain times during the year because of the nature of the business. It might show the actual use of the profits of past years as well as documented plans for future use of accumulated dollars. Corporations that rarely pay dividends are generally suspect, but if the corporation has a strong history of paying dividends, this would be another evidential factor that the current accumulation was not for the prohibited purpose of avoiding personal income tax.

The Internal Revenue Service will give weight to a pattern of expenditures or loans to or on behalf of shareholders to show that the corporation had the financial capacity to distribute retained earnings as dividends but has chosen instead to avoid payment of such funds as dividends in order to prevent personal income taxes at the shareholder level. For the same reason, the Service might question the purpose of corporate funds placed in passive investments, such as the stock of unrelated corporations.

Cheesman: What is the penalty for retaining earnings that are not for the business's needs?

Kress: The penalty for accumulating earnings "beyond the reasonable needs of the business" is as follows: Improper accumulations are taxed at a flat rate of 39.6 percent on all "accumulated taxable income."[34]

It is important to note that the tax, if applicable, is imposed only on *accumulated taxable income,* an amount derived from the taxable income of the corporation for the particular year in question. Thus the tax does not apply to all the accumulated earnings and profits of the corporation but only to the accumulated taxable income of the year or years in which the tax is asserted.

This tax on a corporation's accumulated taxable income is payable in addition to the regular tax payable by the firm. "Accumulated taxable income" basically means the corporation's taxable income for the year in question with certain adjustments (such as a reduction for federal income taxes paid) minus the sum of

- distributions from current earnings and profits that the shareholders have reported as ordinary income (dividends paid), plus
- amounts from earnings and profits that the shareholders have reported as dividends even though no actual distribution was made (disguised dividends), plus

- the accumulated-earnings credit[35]

Keep in mind that in determining whether or not this year's accumulated taxable income has been retained for the reasonable needs of the business, you must also consider the availability of prior years' accumulated earnings. If past years' accumulations are sufficient to meet current needs (that is, this year's business needs) you would have no justification for accumulating this year's earnings.

I just mentioned an accumulated-earnings credit. In Bradwell's case, this is a $250,000 minimum credit, but it is important to note that it includes earnings from prior years. For example, if prior years' accumulated earnings were in excess of $250,000, there would be no credit. Every dollar of this year's accumulated taxable income would be subject to tax, unless it could be proven that the income was reasonable. Let me go into more detail about this credit.

The minimum credit "shall in no case be less than the amount by which $250,000 exceeds the accumulated earnings and profits of the corporation at the close of the preceding taxable year."[36] Thus if the accumulated earnings and profits on December 31 of last year were $20,000, the minimum credit for this year would be $230,000. If no earnings or profits were accumulated in the past, a surplus of at least $250,000 can be accumulated this year without incurring an accumulated-earnings tax. This means that corporations can accumulate up to $250,000 of their earnings and profits without any possibility of being subject to the tax, even though they have no reason for the retention of those earnings. However, that is merely the minimum credit. The maximum credit equals the greater of (1) the minimum credit or (2) the earnings and profits retained for the reasonable needs of the business.

Personal Holding Company Tax

Reebel: Is a personal holding company a tax-avoidance device similar to the unreasonable accumulation of corporate earnings?

Kress: Yes. A personal holding company is a device stockholders have used to place income with a corporation to prevent themselves from being taxed on a personal level. The formulation of a personal holding company generally has taken two forms—the "incorporated-talent" form and the "incorporated-wallet" form. The incorporated-talent or personal-service form of a personal holding company is set up as a result of this type of situation. A highly compensated individual, such as a movie star or athlete, normally receives a very high fee in return for services. This earned income is subject to tax rates of up to 39.6 percent under current law.

Under the incorporated-talents scheme, the financial superstar chose not to receive his or her fee directly, and so formed a corporation and contracted to work for it at a modest, fixed salary. The corporation then contracted the superstar's talents out at the *going rate,* and it received the normally high fee his or her unusual talent brought. Because of the separate entity concept, income attributable to the superstar's services was taxed, not to the individual, but to the corporation at corporate tax rates which were lower than individual rates under prior law. For example, a baseball player would form a corporation and contract to render services to it for, perhaps, $50,000 a year. The corporation would then contract out the player's services for a great deal more, say $120,000 a year. The $70,000 balance would be held and accumulated by the corporation, subject to the lower corporate tax. The corporation could later be liquidated and the individual would pay only a relatively low capital-gain tax on the liquidation.

A second scheme was known as the incorporated-wallet personal holding company. Its purpose was to form a corporation to hold passive investments. Property would be transferred to such a personal holding company so that dividends and interest earned by that property would be taxed at corporate rather than individual rates. The *corporate wallet* would merely hold the assets; collect the dividends, interest, or rental income; and pay tax at relatively lower corporate rates, under prior tax law.

Congress enacted a penalty tax on the undistributed income on corporations that operate as incorporated-talent or incorporated-wallet corporations. In the event that certain mechanical standards of receipt of passive income, personal-service income, and stock ownership found in the Internal Revenue Code are met, such corporations known as personal holding companies will be subject to taxation in addition to the regular corporate taxes.[37] The additional tax imposed is now 39.6 percent of "undistributed personal holding company income," as this is basically taxable income minus taxes paid and dividends distributed.[38]

Baily: When will a corporation be considered a personal holding company?

Kress: To be classified as a personal holding company, two conditions must be present: first, most of the corporation's income (at least 60 percent of *adjusted ordinary gross income*) must come from personal-holding-company passive investment income. Second, more than 50 percent of the value of the stock must be held by five or fewer individuals (this test is broad because ownership attribution rules apply).

Assume Harry Hughes, a billionaire, forms and is the sole shareholder of the Harry Corporation, which holds his large corporate bond portfolio. It will be the policy of the corporation never to distribute dividends. When the Harry Corporation receives the interest, it is taxed at a 39.6 percent rate. However, such a corporation would be found to be a personal holding company under the passive income and stock ownership standards, and Harry Corporation would incur, in addition to the corporate tax, a personal-holding-company penalty tax.

Cheesman: Can the personal-holding-company tax be avoided?

Kress: Yes. The principal way to avoid such a penalty tax is to cause the corporation to distribute dividends. If liability for personal-holding-company tax is found, the Code allows a corporation to mitigate this tax liability by paying a retroactive deficiency dividend.[39] However, liabilities for interest and penalties will not be eliminated. Of course, the distribution of dividends defeats the attempt by taxpayers to have income taxed at lower corporate rates.

Several types of corporations are specifically exempted from the personal-holding-company tax. Among these are life insurance companies, banks, and other financial institutions that are required by law to maintain certain asset reserves.[40]

Reebel: What happens when distributions to shareholders are finally made?

Kress: The taxation of shareholders in this case is the same as under any corporate distribution to shareholders.

Dividend Distributions by the Corporation

Although close corporations are not usually inclined to distribute dividends, a corporation that is already paying the highest reasonable salaries possible must distribute some or all of its profits in the form of dividends. The general rule is that any distribution made by a corporation to its shareholders will be considered a dividend for federal income tax purposes and will be taxed as ordinary income.[41]

There is a limitation on this general rule as well as three basic exceptions. The limitation to the general rule is that a distribution is a taxable dividend only to the extent that it is paid out of either accumulated earnings and profits or current earnings and profits. The three basic exceptions to the general rule are that (1) certain stock dividends are tax free, (2) certain redemptions of stock qualify for capital-gains treatment, and (3) the proceeds of certain liquidations qualify for capital-gains treatment.

Cheesman: I'd like to know more about how we can avoid dividend treatment. Would you discuss these principles in detail?

Kress: Certainly.

First, it might be helpful to discuss exactly how the Code and regulations define the term *dividends.* As I have already mentioned, we start with the general rule that all distributions are dividends. However, there is an *earnings and profits test.* This test provides the tax limit—it tells us how much of any given distribution will be taxable as a dividend and also what portion of that distribution will be considered a tax-free return of capital.[42]

You might think of a corporation as if it were a money machine. We put money into the machine hoping to get a lot more out. Part of the money coming out could be considered earnings and profits, while the balance could be considered part or all that was originally put in. If we think of a corporation this way, then some method has to be devised to determine what portion of a given corporate distribution is taxable at ordinary rates as profit and what portion of each distribution is nontaxable as a return of capital. This is exactly what the tax law gives us—an arbitrary method for distinguishing between (1) what we put in (capital) and (2) what we get out (capital and/or ordinary income and/or capital gains). Therefore some distributions are considered dividends in part, return of capital in part, or even a capital gain in part. Perhaps an example would be helpful.

If current and accumulated earnings and profits are $20,000, and the stockholder's basis for his or her stock is $10,000, a $50,000 distribution would have the following effect:

- To the extent of earnings and profits ($20,000), the distribution is considered a dividend and must be included in the shareholder's gross income.
- Any remaining portion of the distribution has the effect of returning the shareholder's cost. In this case $10,000 of the distribution would be applied against and reduce the shareholder's basis and would therefore be recovered tax free.
- If any portion of the distribution remains, the balance is considered to be a gain from the sale or exchange of property. If the stock was a capital asset in the shareholder's hands and was held for the requisite holding period, long-term capital gain will result. In this example there would be a capital gain of $20,000. (From the $50,000 distribution, $20,000 was applied against earnings and profits and is therefore ordinary income; the next $10,000 was considered a recovery of cost and is therefore tax free; and the remainder, $20,000, is considered gain and will be taxed as a capital gain.)

Baily: What is the effect if the shareholder in this example sells his or her stock after the distribution?

Kress: If the stock is subsequently sold, the stockholder's basis for determining gain or loss on the sale will be zero. Let me point out an important thought on the subject of dividend distributions. When a distribution is made to all shareholders in proportion to the number of shares owned by each shareholder, the distribution will be typically considered a dividend. I want to emphasize that a dividend can be found even in the absence of a formal pro rata distribution. Without any other explanation, the word *dividend* implies any corporate distribution in any form to shareholders from the surplus of the corporation. Therefore ordinary dividends can be paid as cash, notes, or stock of other corporations, or even disguised in various forms.

When a distribution constitutes a dividend, it is taxable as ordinary income to the recipient-shareholder. Note that even though dividends are taxable to the recipient-shareholder, the distributing corporation receives no deduction for the distribution.

When the distribution consists of cash, the amount of cash determines how much taxable income must be reported by the shareholder-recipient. If the dividend is in the form of property, the fair market value of the property determines what is reportable. If the property distributed by the corporation is subject to a liability, the taxable amount is reduced by the amount of liability assumed by the shareholder.

Baily: Will the corporation itself have a gain if it uses appreciated property for corporate distributions?

Kress: The rule is that when appreciated property is distributed in any type of distribution, gain (but not loss) is recognized. This rule is applicable to distributions of dividends and in redemption of stock. The amount realized would be equal to the gain that would have been realized if the property had been sold at the time of the distribution.

Reebel: What effect does a dividend distribution have on the accumulated earnings and profits?

Kress: The accumulated earnings and profits of the corporation will be reduced by the amount of the dividend. When cash is distributed, corporate earnings and profits will be reduced by the amount of that cash. When property other than cash is distributed, the reduction in earnings and profits is measured by the basis of that property to the corporation.

NOTES

1. *Morrisey v. Comm'r,* 296 US 344, 80 L ed 263; and see Treas. Reg. Secs. 301.7701-2 and 301.7701-3.
2. Treas. Reg. Sec. 301.7701-2(d).
3. Treas. Reg. Sec. 301.7701-2(e).
4. Treas. Reg. Sec. 301-7701-2(c).
5. Treas. Reg. Sec. 301-7701-2(b).
6. IRC Secs. 11 and 6012.
7. IRC Secs. 402, 403, 79, 105, and 106.
8. IRC Sec. 162(a).
9. The effect of state corporate taxes should not be overlooked.
10. IRC Secs. 1361-1363; IRC Secs. 1366-1368.
11. IRC Sec. 1374 (tax imposed on certain built-in gains).
12. IRC Sec. 1361(c) and (d).
13. IRC Sec. 1361(b).
14. IRC Sec. 1366(a) and (d).
15. IRC Sec. 1362(d).
16. Reebel, who is transferring cash in exchange for stock, will also receive stock in exchange

for services he is to render to the corporation. The stock he receives will be counted in determining whether the transferors of *property* have control of the corporation. However, the fair market value of the stock he receives for the future performance of services will be currently taxable to him as compensation.

17. IRC Secs. 1001.
18. IRC Sec. 351.
19. IRC Sec. 351(b).
20. IRC Sec. 248. (For purposes of determining the *earnings and profits* of a corporation for dividend payments, organizational expenses are to be capitalized and written off as part of the basis of the corporate asset[s] to which the expenditure applies.)
21. IRC Sec. 385; see also *1988 Tax Guide for Small Business* and *Kraft Foods Co. v. Comm'r,* 232 F.2d 118 (Ratio of Debt to Equity); *J. S. Biritz Construction Company v. Comm'r,* 387 F.2d 454 (Initial Working Capital Requirements); *McSorley's Inc. v. U.S.,* 323 F.2d 900 (Loans Proportionate or Disproportionate to Shareholdings); *Nassau Lens Co. v. Comm'r,* 308 F.2d 39 (Terms of Loan).
22. IRC Sec. 11.
23. IRC Sec. 243.
24. IRC Sec. 162; see also *Chesapeake Mfg. Co., Inc.,* T.C. Memo 1964−214, aff'd. 347 F.2d 507; *R. J. Reynolds Tobacco Co.,* 260 F.2d 9, aff'g. T.C. Memo 1956−161; Treas. Reg. Sec. 1.162-7(b).
25. IRC. Secs. 170 and 162(b).
26. IRC Sec. 1211(a), 1212.
27. IRC Sec. 246.
28. IRC Secs. 531 and 532.
29. IRC Sec. 535(c)(2).
30. IRC Sec. 537; Treas. Reg. Sec. 1.537-1(b)(1) and (2); Treas. Reg. Sec. 1.537-1(a); *Hardin's Bakeries, Inc. v. Martin, Jr.,* D. C. Miss., 1/10/67; Rev. Rul. 67-64, 1967-1 C.B. 150.
31. *General Smelting Co.,* 4 T.C. 313; *Reynard Corp.,* B.T.A. 552; *Harry A. Koch Co. v. Vinal* (Dist. Ct., Neb.) 228 F. Supp. 782; *Vuono-Lione, Inc.,* T.C. Memo 1965-96; *Emeloid Co. v. Comm'r,* 189 F.2d 230; *Bradford-Robinson Printing Co.* (Dist. Ct., Colo., 1958) 1 AFTR 2d 1278.
32. *John P. Scripps Newspapers,* 44 T.C. 453; *Okla. Press Pub. Co. v. U.S.,* 437 F.2d 275; Treas. Reg. Sec. 1.537-2(b)(3).
33. *Mountain State Steel Foundries, Inc. v. Comm'r,* 284 F.2d 737; *Oman Construction Co.,* T.C. Memo 1965-325; *Dill Mfg. Co.,* 39 B.T.A. 1032; *Gazette Publishing Co. v. Self,* 103 F. Supp. 779. See also *Prunier v. Comm'r,* 248 F.2d 818; *Sanders v. Fox,* 253 F.2d 855; *Hedberg-Freidheim Contracting Co.,* T.C. Memo 1956-275, aff'd 25 F.2d 839.
34. IRC Sec. 531.
35. IRC Sec. 535.
36. IRC Sec. 535(c).
37. To be considered personal-service (incorporated-talents) income, the following two tests must be met: (1) the person with whom the corporation has contracted for the services of its "star" has the right to designate that the "star" is the one who must perform the services contracted for, and (2) the individual who must or did perform the services owns 25 percent or more of the stock in the corporation.

In Rev. Rul. 75-67, 1975-9, I.R.B.-7, a doctor, a specialist, incorporated his practice. The Internal Revenue Service ruled that this one-man corporation would not be considered a personal holding company as long as the doctor was not designated orally or in writing to personally perform services, and the services would not be so unique as to preclude substitution.

38. IRC Sec. 541.
39. IRC Sec. 547.
40. IRC Sec. 542(c) and (d).
41. IRC Secs. 301 and 316.
42. IRC Secs. 301 and 316(a); Treas. Reg. Sec. 1.316-1(a) and (c).

11

Taxation of Stock Redemptions and Rules for Constructive Ownership

James F. Ivers III and Ted Kurlowicz*

Many problems in financial and estate planning for shareholders in closely held corporations can be solved through redemptions of some or all of their stock. The Internal Revenue Code defines a redemption of stock as an acquisition by a corporation of its own stock from a shareholder "in exchange for property, whether or not stock so acquired is canceled, retired, or held as Treasury stock."

In many states local law provides that a corporation cannot purchase its own stock without adequate surplus funds. For this reason the planner should be aware of local corporation law, including how it determines the amount of a corporation's surplus, whenever a redemption of stock is considered.

For tax planning purposes the primary objective in arranging a stock redemption is to achieve capital-gain treatment as opposed to dividend treatment on the exchange of stock for money or other property. If the transaction is treated as a dividend distribution rather than as a capital transaction, the redemption proceeds will be taxable as ordinary income.

Capital transactions are subject to tax treatment that is more favorable than the treatment that applies to dividends. First, an individual's capital losses are deductible in full against capital gains for any given year. On the other hand, net capital losses are deductible against ordinary income only to the extent of $3,000 per year. Capital losses, therefore, can "shelter" capital gains fully. Second, in a capital transaction a taxpayer receives back his or her basis as a tax-free return of capital when property is sold. This can be very important, for example, if a shareholder's basis in redeemed stock is high. Of course, return of basis is much less significant if the redeemed shareholder's basis in the shares is very low. Third, long-term capital gains are now subject to a maximum statutory marginal tax rate of 28 percent. The maximum marginal rate applicable to ordinary income is currently 39.6 percent.

It is important to note in this context that an estate receives a stepped-up basis in a decedent's stock that is generally equal to the value of the stock at the

---

*Ted Kurlowicz, JD, LLM, CLU, ChFC, is professor of taxation at The American College.

date of the decedent's death. Therefore the qualification of a redemption from an estate as a capital transaction is very important. Stock redemptions from estates that qualify as capital transactions will usually provide little or no income tax liability because the redemption price will be approximately equal to the estate's basis in the decedent's stock.

On the other hand, if a stock redemption from a decedent's estate is treated as a dividend, the estate's stepped-up basis in the stock is ignored, and the full amount of the redemption proceeds will be taxed as a dividend to the extent of the corporation's earnings and profits.

This chapter will first examine the technical requirements for qualifying a redemption as a capital transaction. Then planning opportunities that the tax law presents in this area will be explored.

GENERAL RULES FOR TAXATION OF CORPORATE DISTRIBUTIONS

Unless the Internal Revenue Code provides otherwise, a distribution of property from a corporation to a shareholder is treated as a dividend to the extent of the corporation's current and accumulated earnings and profits. "Earnings and profits" are computed according to tax accounting principles. It may be said that the earnings and profits of a corporation for a given taxable year are determined by reference to the corporation's taxable income. However, several significant positive and negative adjustments to taxable income are made to determine the amount of earnings and profits for tax purposes. The specific adjustments are beyond the scope of this reading.

However, if a distribution that would otherwise be taxable as a dividend is in excess of the corporation's earnings and profits, the amount distributed by the corporation in excess of its earnings and profits is treated as a capital transaction. That is, the amount in excess is treated as a return of capital to the extent of the shareholder's basis in the stock. The balance, if any, will be treated as capital gain.

> *Example:* Linda is the sole shareholder in the Allston Corporation, which has $40,000 in current and accumulated earnings and profits. Linda's basis in her Allston stock is $6,000. The corporation distributes to Linda $50,000, which is not compensation for her services. Of this amount Linda must treat $40,000 as a dividend, taxable as ordinary income. The next $6,000 of the distribution is treated as a return of Linda's capital investment in the Allston stock. Her basis in the stock is thereby reduced to zero. The remaining $4,000 of the distribution will be treated as capital gain.

REDEMPTIONS THAT ARE TAXED AS CAPITAL TRANSACTIONS

As already stated, the general rule provides that dividend treatment is applied to the proceeds of a redemption to the extent of the corporation's current and accumulated earnings and profits. However, the tax law provides exceptions to the general rule. These exceptions apply to certain types of redemptions in which the redeemed shareholder's percentage of ownership of the corporation is materially affected by the redemption. These types of redemptions are treated as capital transactions rather than as dividend distributions.

One type of redemption treated under the general rule is a pro rata redemption. A redemption that is pro rata among shareholders does not change the percentages of ownership, so the redeemed shareholder's percentage of ownership is not affected.

> *Example:* Two shareholders each own a 50 percent interest in a corporation, and the corporation redeems half of each shareholder's stock. After the redemption both shareholders still have the same proportionate interest in the corporation that they had before the redemption. The ownership of the corporation has not been materially affected by the transaction. Therefore the proceeds will be treated as a dividend distribution to the extent of current and accumulated earnings and profits.

The Internal Revenue Code contains specific provisions describing certain types of redemptions that materially affect a shareholder's percentage of ownership. If a given redemption qualifies under one of these provisions, the transaction will be treated as a capital transaction for tax purposes. Sec. 302 allows such treatment for the following four types of redemptions:

- a redemption that is "not essentially equivalent to a dividend"
- a "substantially disproportionate" redemption
- a "complete" redemption
- a distribution to a noncorporate shareholder in "partial liquidation" of the distributing corporation

Redemptions Not Essentially Equivalent to a Dividend

This first category involves questions of fact. Each redemption for which a taxpayer seeks treatment under this provision must be evaluated according to its particular facts if the IRS challenges capital-gain treatment claimed by the redeemed shareholder. There are several revenue rulings in which the IRS has conceded that certain redemptions resulted in a "meaningful reduction" in a shareholder's interest in a corporation. A meaningful reduction is required for a redemption to be considered not essentially equivalent to a dividend. This is not a mathematical test, but a subjective one.

Substantially Disproportionate Redemptions

The second category under Sec. 302 is that of a substantially disproportionate redemption. Sec. 302 provides for automatic qualification of a substantially disproportionate redemption as a capital transaction if a mathematical safe-harbor test is met. The test defines a substantially disproportionate redemption as follows:

- After the redemption the shareholder must own less than 50 percent of the total voting power of the corporation.
- The shareholder's percentage ownership of *voting* stock of the corporation after the redemption must be less than 80 percent of his or her percentage ownership of voting stock before the redemption.
- The shareholder's percentage ownership of *common* stock of the corporation after the redemption must also be less than 80 percent of his or her percentage ownership of common stock before the redemption.

Example: Sobel and Sherman (unrelated individuals) each own 400 of the 800 outstanding voting common shares of Thor Industries, Inc. Thor has no other classes of stock outstanding. A proposal is made to redeem 300 of Sobel's shares. Under the test for substantially disproportionate redemptions the following results occur:

- After the redemption Sobel will own 100 of the 500 outstanding Thor shares. This is less than 50 percent, so the first test is met.
- Before the redemption Sobel's interest was 50 percent of Thor. Eighty percent of 50 percent is 40 percent. After the redemption Sobel's interest will be 20 percent of Thor (100 of the 500 outstanding voting common shares). Since this is less than 40 percent, the 80 percent test is met for both voting and common stock, since only one class of stock is outstanding.

The redemption will qualify as substantially disproportionate.

It is important to note that for purposes of the 80 percent test, the shareholder's proportionate percentage of ownership is the ratio of his or her shares owned to the total shares outstanding. Therefore both parts of the ratio will change after the redemption. The postredemption ratio must reflect the reduction in the total number of shares outstanding. The planner should multiply the preredemption ratio of ownership by 80 percent. Any postredemption ratio that is less than 80 percent of the preredemption ratio is an acceptable reduction of percentage ownership under the 80 percent test.

Complete Redemptions

A complete termination of the shareholder's interest in the redeeming corporation is the third category under Sec. 302. To qualify for capital treatment under this category, the corporation must redeem all the stock the shareholder owns. If the redemption is a complete redemption, it will be treated in its entirety as a capital transaction.

Partial Liquidations

The fourth category under Sec. 302 is that of a distribution in which there is partial liquidation of the distributing corporation. In determining whether a redemption qualifies under this category, the nature of the distribution must be examined at the corporate level, rather than from the point of view of the shareholder receiving proceeds. Distributions in partial liquidation are beyond the scope of this reading.

ATTRIBUTION OF STOCK OWNERSHIP

Attribution of ownership means that stock owned by one individual or entity is considered to be owned by another individual or entity for the purpose of determining how a particular transaction is taxed.

In evaluating a redemption under each of the first three categories described above, the rules for attribution of stock ownership must be considered. Attribution may adversely affect the tax treatment of a redemption. Also referred to as constructive ownership, attribution can cause a redemption that would otherwise be taxable as a capital transaction to be treated as a dividend distribution to the extent of the corporation's current and accumulated earnings and profits, since attribution changes a shareholder's percentage of ownership for purposes of determining the tax effects of a redemption.

The rationale for attribution of ownership is that a shareholder may effectively control the operation of a corporation through shares owned by related individuals and entities as well as through shares he or she actually owns. Although this may not in fact be true in many instances, redemptions should always be structured to comply with the attribution rules when these rules are applicable.

Any redemption involving stock of a corporation owned by related parties should be evaluated with these rules in mind.

Family Attribution

Stock owned by an individual shareholder's parents, spouse, children, and grandchildren will be attributed to the shareholder for purposes of determining the tax treatment of a redemption. Stock owned by the shareholder's grandparents or siblings will not be attributed. There is a rationale for these distinctions. In most instances dealings between siblings are more likely to be at arm's length than are dealings between parent and child or between spouses. In addition, it is a more natural situation for stock of a grandparent to pass to a grandchild and remain effectively controlled by the grandparent than for a grandchild to attempt to effectively exercise rights of ownership in stock owned by a grandparent.

Attribution from an Entity

In general, ownership of stock is attributed to a shareholder from an entity in proportion to the shareholder's interest in the entity. However, partnerships, estates, trusts, and corporations are all treated somewhat differently in the application of this general rule.

Attribution from Partnerships

If a partnership owns stock in a corporation, a partner is deemed to own that amount of stock owned by the partnership that is in proportion to the partner's interest in the partnership.

> *Example:* The Hamilton partnership owns 100 shares in Commonwealth Realty Corporation. Harold is a 50 percent partner in Hamilton and owns 100 shares in Commonwealth Realty, which redeems 25 of Harold's shares. For purposes of determining the tax treatment of Harold's redemption, Harold is also deemed to own 50 of the 100 shares in Commonwealth Realty owned by the Hamilton partnership.

Attribution from Estates

The general rule that ownership of stock is attributed to a shareholder from an entity in proportion to the shareholder's interest in the entity applies to attribution from an estate to a beneficiary of the estate. However, the beneficiary must have a direct present interest in the estate for attribution to occur. An individual holding a remainder interest in an estate would not have ownership of stock attributed from the estate. Also after an estate has completed its distribution of property to a beneficiary, any stock still owned by the estate will generally no longer be attributed to the beneficiary.

Attribution from Trusts

To determine whether stock owned by a trust is attributable to a trust beneficiary, another variation of the general rule is applied. An actuarial computation of a beneficiary's interest in a trust is made to determine the percentage of stock owned by the trust that will be attributed to the beneficiary. Therefore a beneficiary having only a remainder interest in a trust is subject to attribution of ownership from the trust, even though a remainder interest in an estate would not result in attribution to the beneficiary from the estate.

Attribution from Corporations

The general rule also applies in attributing ownership of stock from a corporation to a shareholder of the corporation, with one important modification. Stock ownership will be attributed from a corporation to a shareholder only if the shareholder is a 50-percent-or-greater owner of the value of all the outstanding stock of the corporation that owns the stock to be attributed.

> *Example:* Suppose Kevin is a 60 percent owner of the Building Corporation and also owns stock in the Hammer and Nail Corporation. The Building Corporation is also a shareholder in the Hammer and Nail Corporation. When the Hammer and Nail Corporation redeems a portion of Kevin's shares, 60 percent of the stock in Hammer and Nail owned by the Building Corporation will be attributed to Kevin for purposes of determining the tax treatment of Kevin's redemption. However, if Kevin were only a 49 percent owner of the Building Corporation, the stock in Hammer and Nail owned by Building would not be attributed to Kevin when Hammer and Nail redeems a portion of Kevin's shares.

Special Rule for S Corporations

It is important to note that the stock attribution rules treat an S corporation as if it were a partnership. Therefore to determine the attribution of stock ownership both to an S corporation and from an S corporation, the rules that apply to partnerships must be used.

Attribution to an Entity

When a corporation redeems shares owned by a partnership, estate, trust, or another corporation, the attribution rules must be examined to determine the tax treatment of the entity receiving proceeds of the redemption.

In general, all the stock owned by a partner, a beneficiary of an estate or trust, or a controlling shareholder in a corporation will be attributed to the partnership, estate, trust, or corporation.

> *Example:* The Horseshoe Corporation redeems stock owned by the Trail partnership. Marjorie, a partner in Trail, also owns stock in the Horseshoe Corporation. For purposes of determining the tax treatment of the redemption of Trail's stock in Horseshoe, Trail is deemed to own the stock in Horseshoe owned by Marjorie.

There are modifications to this general rule that apply to trusts and to corporations.

Stock owned by a contingent beneficiary of a trust will not be attributed to a trust if, considering the trustee's discretionary powers under the trust instrument, the beneficiary's largest potential interest in the value of the trust property, determined actuarially, is 5 percent or less of the value of the trust property.

Stock in one corporation owned by a shareholder who also owns stock in a second corporation will not be attributed to the second corporation unless the shareholder owns 50 percent or more of the value of the second corporation that is receiving proceeds of a redemption by the first corporation.

> *Example:* Paul is a 40 percent owner of Landscape Corporation. Both Paul and Landscape Corporation own stock in the Tractor Corporation. Tractor redeems the Tractor stock owned by Landscape. To determine the tax treatment to Landscape in this transaction, stock in Tractor owned by Paul is not considered to be owned by Landscape since Paul owns less than 50 percent of Landscape.

Note how attribution *to* a corporation is different from attribution *from* a corporation. A corporation is deemed to own *all* the stock in another corporation owned by one of its shareholders if attribution applies. However, attribution of stock from a corporation to a shareholder receiving proceeds of a redemption by another corporation applies only to the extent of the shareholder's percentage interest in the corporation from which ownership is attributed.

> *Example:* Suppose Paul in the above example is a 50 percent owner of Landscape Corporation. Paul and Landscape each own 100 shares of

the Tractor Corporation. If Tractor redeems Landscape's stock in Tractor, Landscape will be considered to own all 100 shares in Tractor owned by Paul. However, if Tractor redeems Paul's stock in Tractor, Paul will be considered to own only 50 of the shares in Tractor owned by Landscape.

Reattribution

The term *reattribution* refers to situations in which constructive ownership rules are combined to attribute ownership from one shareholder to another shareholder not directly related under the rules.

Example: A father will be considered to own the stock owned by a trust of which his son is the sole beneficiary.

Example: A corporation will be considered to own 50 percent of the stock owned by a partnership in which the corporation's sole shareholder is a 50 percent partner.

There are certain situations in which the Internal Revenue Code prohibits reattribution. For instance, family ownership rules cannot be applied two times in succession.

Example: A father will be considered to own stock owned by his son. Likewise, a daughter will be considered to own stock owned by her father. However, family attribution rules cannot be applied twice in succession to attribute ownership of the son's stock to the daughter. If this type of constructive ownership applied, it would result in sibling attribution.

Waiver of Family Attribution in Complete Redemptions

If a corporation redeems all the stock owned by a shareholder, it is possible for the shareholder to avoid the application of the family attribution rules. In order to qualify for a waiver of family attribution in a complete redemption, a shareholder must comply with a number of requirements imposed by the Internal Revenue Code. These include the following:

- The redeemed shareholder may retain no interest in the corporation after the redemption. For these purposes "interest" includes the status of officer, director, or employee of the corporation. It is permissible for the redeemed shareholder to remain a creditor of the corporation.

- The redeemed shareholder must not acquire any prohibited interest in the corporation for a period of 10 years beginning on the date of the distribution of the redemption proceeds. However, if the redeemed shareholder receives stock in the corporation by bequest or inheritance, this provision is not violated.
- The redeemed shareholder must file an agreement with the IRS to notify it if any acquisition of a prohibited interest takes place within the 10-year period. The redeemed shareholder must retain the necessary records to comply with this requirement.
- The redeemed shareholder must not have acquired any portion of the stock redeemed during a 10-year period prior to the date of the redemption from a person whose stock would be attributable to the redeemed shareholder.
- The redeemed shareholder must not have transferred any stock in the redeeming corporation to any person whose stock would be attributed to the redeemed shareholder within a 10-year period before the date of distribution of the redemption proceeds. This requirement will not apply if the corporation also redeems such stock of the person to whom it was transferred by the redeemed shareholder.

The last two requirements may not apply if the redeemed shareholder can show that the transfer or acquisition in question did not have the avoidance of federal income tax as one of its principal purposes. The waiver of attribution is available only in the case of a complete redemption and generally only for the family attribution rules (not entity attribution).

However, an entity (estate, partnership, trust, or corporation) can also make use of the waiver-of-family attribution provisions, as long as all individuals whose stock would be attributable to the entity comply with the conditions for waiver of family attribution. Note, however, that waiver by an estate has limited application because in most cases stock in a family corporation will be owned by family members or left to family members under the decedent's will, so that beneficiaries of the estate will also be stockholders. Still, in certain situations an estate may be able to effectively claim the waiver.

> *Example:* The Connecticut Corporation plans to redeem its stock owned by Biff's estate. Biff's estate is a 50 percent shareholder in Connecticut. The other 50 percent of Connecticut is owned by Bunny, Bill's wife. Biff and Bunny's son and daughter, Rollo and Muffy, are the sole beneficiaries of Biff's estate. Biff's estate can achieve capital-gain treatment on the redemption of Connecticut stock through the waiver-of-family attribution rules as long as Rollo and Muffy agree not to acquire any interest in the corporation that is prohibited by those rules during the

time period prescribed by the rules. In effect, the waiver-of-family attribution rules in this situation operate as if the beneficiaries of the estate were the parties whose stock was redeemed.

SEC. 303 REDEMPTIONS

The Internal Revenue Code contains a relief provision that applies to estates in which stock of a closely held corporation constitutes a substantial portion of total estate assets. The purpose of this section is to provide liquidity for such estates in order to avoid forced sales of the closely held stock to meet tax obligations and administration expenses.

This relief provision, Sec. 303 of the Code, allows distributions in redemption of such stock to be treated as made in exchange for a capital asset and therefore eligible for capital-gains treatment, subject to certain requirements and limitations. Sec. 303 is totally independent of the other Code provisions describing the tax treatment of redemptions of stock. Therefore neither the rules under Sec. 302 nor the constructive ownership rules need to be considered in determining whether favorable tax treatment is available under Sec. 303. Sec. 303 operates independently, and as long as its own requirements are met, favorable tax treatment can be achieved.

What Estates May Qualify under Sec. 303?

In order for an estate to be eligible for a Sec. 303 redemption, the value of corporate stock includible in the gross estate for federal estate tax purposes must be more than 35 percent of the value of the adjusted gross estate. The adjusted gross estate is defined for this purpose as the gross estate less deductions for funeral and administration expenses, debts, and deductible losses of the estate. To determine whether the corporate stock meets the percentage test, all classes of stock in the corporation owned by the estate are counted; that is, preferred is counted as well as common.

For estates that own stock in two or more corporations there is a variation of the 35 percent test. If the stock in the two or more corporations owned by the estate represent 20 percent or more of the outstanding value of all the stock in each corporation, the stock in the two or more corporations may be combined and treated as stock in one corporation for purposes of the 35 percent test. If the test is met by combining stock in two or more corporations, a Sec. 303 redemption may be made with shares of any of the two or more corporations.

Example: Spike's estate needs liquidity to meet its tax obligations and administration expenses. The estate owns 100 shares in the Jersey Video Corporation. These shares represent 25 percent of the value of Spike's adjusted gross estate and 33 percent of the value of Jersey Video, Inc. The estate also owns 100 shares in Philly Stereo, Inc. These shares represent 15 percent of the value of Spike's adjusted gross estate and 25 percent of the value of Philly Stereo, Inc. Because the stock in each corporation owned by the estate represents 20 percent or more of the value of the stock in each corporation, and because the stock in the two corporations has a total value in excess of 35 percent of Spike's adjusted gross estate, the estate will qualify for a Sec. 303 redemption.

There is one further wrinkle that applies *only* to the special rule for stock in two or more corporations. For purposes of the 20 percent requirement 100 percent of the value of stock the decedent held with his or her surviving spouse as community property or in joint tenancy, tenancy by the entirety, or tenancy in common is treated as having been included in the decedent's gross estate. This wrinkle applies *only* when the rule for stock in two or more corporations is applied and not to the 35 percent test in general.

How Much Stock May Be Redeemed under Sec. 303?

There is a limitation on the dollar amount of proceeds received for redeemed stock that will qualify for favorable treatment under Sec. 303. Redemption proceeds eligible for favorable tax treatment may not exceed the sum of the estate, inheritance, legacy, and succession taxes for which the estate is liable (including interest, if any) and the amount of funeral and administration expenses allowable as deductions to the estate under the Internal Revenue Code.

The amount of proceeds qualifying for treatment under Sec. 303 will be further limited if the redeemed shareholder (usually the estate) is not legally liable for the full amount of the taxes and expenses. Only that portion of the taxes and expenses that the redeemed shareholder is legally obligated to pay is considered in determining the maximum amount of proceeds allowable under Sec. 303.

Example: A trust owns stock in the Texas Corporation that is included in Alvin's gross estate. The trust instrument does not require the trust to pay a portion of the taxes or administration expenses of Alvin's estate. However, Fergus, the trustee, uses proceeds of a redemption of the trust's stock in Texas to pay a portion of Alvin's estate taxes. In this situation the trust may not treat the redemption under Sec. 303.

Who May Receive Favorable Tax Treatment under Sec. 303?

If the requirements of Sec. 303 are met, any shareholder owning stock included in determining a decedent's gross estate is eligible for a Sec. 303 redemption. Generally the eligible shareholder will be either the decedent's estate itself or a beneficiary of the estate. However, in this context it is important to remember that unless a beneficiary of the estate has an obligation to pay death taxes or administration expenses, the beneficiary will not be eligible for Sec. 303 treatment.

When Must a Sec. 303 Redemption Be Made?

Sec. 303 treatment is available for distributions in redemption of stock made after the decedent's death and within 3 years and 90 days after the filing of the estate's federal estate tax return. If the estate has filed a petition in the Tax Court concerning an estate tax dispute, the time limitation is extended until 60 days after the decision of the Tax Court becomes final. Furthermore, if the estate has elected to pay its estate tax in installments under Sec. 6166 of the Internal Revenue Code, redemption distributions may receive the benefit of Sec. 303 if they are made within the time period of the installment payments.

Under any of these rules if redemption proceeds are paid more than 4 years after the death of the decedent, the amount of distributions eligible to be treated under Sec. 303 cannot exceed the lesser of the amount of taxes and administration expenses remaining unpaid or the amount of such expenses that are paid within one year after the redemption.

Planning Considerations under Sec. 303

Minimal Taxable Gain

Because of its fiduciary duties to its other shareholders, a corporation will generally redeem the stock of a decedent shareholder at a price equal to the stock's current fair market value. For income tax purposes an estate or its beneficiary receives a "stepped-up" basis in a decedent's assets that is generally equal to the value of the assets as of the date of the decedent's death. Therefore if a redemption is made under Sec. 303 within a short time after the decedent's death, the redemption price should be equal to or very close to the basis in the stock held by the estate or the beneficiary. Since proceeds in a Sec. 303 redemption are treated as received in the sale or exchange of a capital asset, and not as a dividend, there will generally be little or no taxable gain realized by the redeemed shareholder. If the stock has increased in value between the time of the decedent's death and the time of the redemption, any amount in excess of the estate's or beneficiary's basis in the stock will be taxed as long-term capital gain. Therefore unless there has been a significant change in the corporation's fortunes during that time, the amount of taxable gain will probably not be significant.

Accumulated-Earnings Tax

One problem that may arise in planning for the corporation to fund a Sec. 303 redemption is the accumulated-earnings tax. The Internal Revenue Code states specifically that corporate accumulations may be made to fund a Sec. 303 redemption without being subject to the accumulated-earnings tax. However, such accumulations are specifically exempt only when made in the taxable year of the corporation in which the decedent died or any taxable year thereafter. Therefore accumulations prior to the year of the decedent's death to meet an anticipated funding need for a redemption may present the corporation with an accumulated-earnings tax problem. This problem is amplified by the requirement mentioned earlier that in some states a redemption may be effected only if the corporation has adequate surplus to fund the redemption.

If the IRS can show that the funding objective was not for a corporate purpose, but only for the benefit of the shareholder or the shareholder's estate, the accumulated-earnings tax may become a problem. It may be difficult to convince the IRS that a Sec. 303 redemption serves a business purpose of the corporation. Therefore as a practical matter the use of life insurance owned by the corporation may be the most appropriate method of funding a Sec. 303 redemption. Even though the accumulation of earnings to meet premium obligations for such insurance may be subject to the accumulated-earnings tax, the dollar amount needed for premiums will be substantially less than the dollar amount needed for cash funding. As a result, any possible exposure to the accumulated-earnings tax is minimized. The proper life insurance funding will also provide any surplus required to effect the redemption.

12

An Overview of the Income Taxation of Partners and Partnerships

Stephan R. Leimberg, Michael R. Harris,
and Frank Vallei[*]

In order to highlight some of the more essential areas of partnership taxation, the following reading is written as a narrative between a CLU, an attorney, and a CPA. Because of the complexity of partnership taxation, the subject matter covered should be considered merely an introductory overview.

More specific information on the topics covered can be found in Stanley and Kilcullen's Federal Income Tax Law *under the appropriate Code sections and in the* Tax Guide for Small Business *available from the Internal Revenue Service.*

Tax Law Definition of a Partnership

Steve: Mike, what is a partnership for tax law purposes?

Mike: That's not such an easy question. The Internal Revenue Code defines a partnership to include ". . . a syndicate, group, pool, joint venture, or other unincorporated organization, through or by means of which any business, financial operation, or venture is carried on, and which is not within the meaning of this title, a trust or estate or a corporation: . . ."[1]

Identifying a trust or estate is usually not a major problem. It is sometimes difficult, however, to make the distinction between an organization that is—and therefore should be taxed as—a corporation and one that is a partnership. Just because a business calls itself a partnership, or files partnership returns, or is a partnership under state law, does not mean it will be taxed as a partnership. And as you can see, the Code definition is not much help.

The Treasury regulations offer a little more guidance.[2] They set out six characteristics of corporate existence that are applied to distinguish between an

---

[*]Michael R. Harris is in the private practice of law and is a member of the Montgomery County Bar Association. Frank Vallei is a certified public accountant and maintains a practice in both Pennsylvania and New Jersey. His main office is in Bala Cynwyd, Pennsylvania. This reading has been updated by James F. Ivers III.

organization taxable as a corporation and one taxable as a partnership. These characteristics are

1. associates
2. an objective to carry on business and divide the gain therefrom
3. continuity of life
4. centralization of management
5. limited liability (limited to the entity's property)
6. free transferability of interests

Characteristics (1) and (2) are common to both corporations and partnerships. The regulations accordingly say to ignore these factors and determine whether a majority of factors (3) to (6) are present. If they are, then the entity is a corporation for federal tax purposes. If they are not, then a partnership *may* exist.

To be confident your business activity will be taxed as a partnership rather than a corporation, it should have at least two of the following characteristics:

- an absence of continuity of life (under state law, a partnership is dissolved by the death or withdrawal of a partner even though it may not terminate for income tax purposes)[3]
- a lack of centralized management (in a partnership each partner may act on behalf of the partnership)[4]
- unlimited liability of the partners[5]
- inability of the partners to freely transfer interests (a general partner may not transfer an interest without the other partners' unanimous consent)

The federal tax treatment of a business entity is a separate determination from how the entity is formed under state law. For example, a limited-liability company (LLC) is a type of business entity formed under state law, not federal tax law. Most LLCs are taxed as partnerships under federal tax law because they do not have sufficient corporate characteristics for tax purposes.

Steve: You mentioned that an organization not classified as a corporation for tax purposes *may* be considered a partnership. What else could it be?

Mike: It is possible for the entity to be neither a partnership nor a corporation, despite the fact that several individuals are involved in a profit-motivated enterprise. This situation arises mainly in investment-motivated joint ventures.

For example, Tony and Carol are co-owners of the Metropolitan building. This co-ownership alone does not make the relationship between Tony and Carol a partnership. Likewise, an agreement between Tony and Carol to share expenses is not a partnership. A partnership exists only where the parties actively carry on a trade, business, or financial operation and intend to divide the profits and losses. If Tony and Carol also leased space in their building and provided substantial services to their tenants (and both intended to share profits and losses), a partnership between Tony and Carol would exist.

Importance of Characterization as a Partnership

Steve: Why is it important that we know how a given organization will be characterized?

Frank: Perhaps the most important reason is that taxation follows characterization, and it is important that a particular organization be taxed as the parties involved intended. The distinction between a corporation and a partnership is a good illustration.

When the organization is taxed as a corporation, the organization and its members are treated as two separate and distinct taxable entities.[6]

When profits are earned by a corporation, they are taxed once to the business and then taxed again to the shareholders if they are paid out in the form of dividends. This potential double taxation is avoided in a partnership. A great many states also tax both the income of a corporation and the dividends received by its shareholders. If the organization is considered a partnership, these same profits earned by the same recipients will be taxed only once—on the recipients' individual returns. If a business is classified as a corporation, losses may be claimed only by the corporation and are not available to offset the shareholder's other income. In the event that the partnership has a net loss, the partners take their share of the loss on their individual returns. As a practical matter, the IRS will usually attempt to tax an unincorporated organization as a corporation only in cases involving limited partnerships in which investor limited partners have sought to deduct losses on their individual returns.

The Aggregate and Entity Theories

Steve: Am I correct in thinking that there is no difference between partners and their partnership—so that for tax purposes a partnership is equivalent to the sum of its individual members?

Mike: This statement is only partially correct. Woven into the relevant sections of the Internal Revenue Code are two general theories used in developing the tax law relating to partnerships and their partners. These are called the "aggregate" theory and the "entity" theory.

According to the aggregate theory, a partnership is considered as an aggregate of individual co-owners who have bound themselves together with the intention of sharing gains and losses. The key point here is that under the aggregate theory, the partnership itself has no existence separate and apart from its members. As the word aggregate implies, to the extent this theory influences tax law, a partnership is nothing more than the sum of its individual members.

The Code recognizes this theory by requiring that each partner include on his or her personal income tax return his or her share of certain partnership gains, losses, deductions, and credits. This means that it is not the partnership that is taxable. Rather, it is the partners who are subject to the income tax as an aggregate of individuals. In other words, the individual partners are the taxpayers, not the partnership.

At the same time, however, the Code provides that for certain other purposes, the partnership is a separate entity that is distinct from its members. Accordingly, the partnership must file an income tax return for information purposes only—Form 1065—and show gross income, business deductions, and taxable income.

Three other indicia of the entity theory are that a partnership has a taxable year, its own accounting method, and the right to exercise various income tax elections.

Steve: Would you explain the aggregate and entity theories in more detail?

Mike: Let me start with the aggregate theory. According to the aggregate theory, since a partnership is not a separate entity, no tax is imposed on the partnership itself. The liability is instead passed through directly to each partner who pays tax on his or her share of the profits just as though he or she realized the share of income as an individual. Capital gains, Section 1231 gains, dividends, and other taxable items are also passed directly through to the partners, who add them to like items on their 1040s.

In keeping this *conduit* concept, these items retain their character. For example, as capital gains flow through the partnership conduit to the taxpaying partners, the aggregate theory keeps the nature of the gain the same—capital gain.

However, even while the aggregate theory makes the partnership a conduit for some purposes, the entity theory treats the partnership as separate from its individual partners. The entity theory requires the partnership itself to file a return. The return provides a way to inform both the IRS and the individual partners how the profits and losses are allocated.

For example, the partnership return breaks down the partnership's ordinary taxable income or loss, its net capital gain or loss, its Section 1231 gains or losses, its charitable contributions, and its receipt of dividends. Then each partner can readily see from his or her separate Schedule K-1 on Form 1065 his or her share of the partnership's income, credits, deductions, and so forth.

Another good example of the entity theory is the way partners who deal with their own partnership are treated. Generally a partner who engages in a transaction with his or her partnership is treated taxwise like a stranger. This rule does not apply to certain sales or exchanges of property between partners and partnerships. This means that when a partner is not acting in his or her capacity as a partner, a transaction between that partner and the partnership is treated as if it was conducted between the partnership and an unrelated third person.

For example, Debra and Lillian form a partnership with equal capital and income interests. The partnership agrees to pay Debra, the working member, $10,000 a year as salary. If the income (after deductions for expenses other than salaries) of the partnership is $10,000 and that entire amount is paid to Debra, she has taxable income of $10,000. The partnership itself has no taxable income. But if that same partnership had income after deductions (other than the salary deduction) of $25,000, Debra would be taxable on $17,500. That $17,500 would be composed of $10,000 of salary and Debra's distributive share of the partnership's taxable income. Her distributive share is one-half of $15,000, that is, one-half of the $25,000 of partnership income (after deductions other than salary), less the business expense deduction of $10,000 for the salary paid to Debra.

Other instances occur where a partner dealing with the partnership is treated as if he or she was not a partner when the partner lends money or property to the partnership or purchases property from the partnership.[7]

Tax Ramifications in the Formation of a Partnership

Steve: I know that it is possible to form a corporation without incurring a tax even if the members contribute appreciated property. Can you explain the tax ramifications of forming a partnership?

Frank: Say you and I are both engaged in the same type of work. We agree it would be mutually beneficial to pool our talents, money, and other property. We might just shake hands or we might draw up a formal agreement that allocates partnership income, deductions, gain, loss, and credits. Any fees paid in connection with the organization, such as legal fees, are considered capital expenditures that may be amortized and deducted over a 5-year period.

We agree to form an equal partnership. You contribute $24,000 in cash—I'll contribute a building with a fair market value of $24,000. Generally speaking, no gain or loss is recognized on the exchange of property or money for an interest in a partnership.[8]

Assume my building, valued at $24,000, has a basis depreciated to $10,000. I've realized a $14,000 gain on the trade of my title to the building for a partnership interest. But I don't have to recognize that gain for tax purposes.

Instead, the basis for my partnership interest remains the same as the basis I had in the property I contributed, or $10,000.[9] If I should immediately sell my partnership interest for $18,000, I'd have an $8,000 gain. So the general rule is this: The basis a contributing partner had for property he or she contributes to the partnership becomes his or her initial basis for his or her partnership interest. Stated more precisely, the amount of cash contributed plus the adjusted basis an individual had in the contributed property becomes the original basis for his or her new partnership interest.

When contributed property is subject to indebtedness, the original basis of the contributor's partnership interest must be lowered by the portion of the indebtedness taken over by the other partners.[10] So if the $10,000 property I contribute is subject to a $6,000 lien, and the partnership assumes this liability, the basis for my partnership interest will be reduced to the extent that you assume part of this $6,000 liability. In this example, being an equal partner, you'd assume half of the liability, so my basis would drop from $10,000 to $7,000. If you contributed $7,000 in cash, your basis would be the $7,000 you contributed plus the $3,000 share of the liability you assumed, for a total basis of $10,000. Note that if the property contributed to the partnership is subject to a liability in excess of its basis in the hands of the contributing partner, more complex tax problems arise and the contributing partner may realize taxable gain.

The partnership's basis in contributed property is the same as the contributing partner's basis in the asset. Therefore in the previous example, the partnership would have a $10,000 basis in the property I contributed. If the partnership later sells the property for $20,000, the partnership has a taxable gain of $10,000. Note that there is a distinction between a partner's basis in his or her partnership interest and the partnership's basis in assets contributed by its partners.

Now I might not have cash to contribute—but I do have unique talents I can bring into the business. If I contributed property in return for my partnership interest, I would not have to recognize either gain or loss. But if I contribute either past services or the promise of future services, this general rule doesn't apply.

The receipt of an interest in partnership capital in return for services is regarded by the tax law as compensation for services rendered (or to be rendered).[11] So I may have to pay a current tax on the fair market value of the interest in partnership capital I receive in return for my services.

Sometimes an interest in partnership capital will be transferred to an individual subject to the condition that he or she must complete specified services at a future date. For example, you and I could form a partnership. You provide cash and I provide talent. You transfer an interest in the partnership capital to me conditioned on my completion of 5 years of service. I will realize income as soon as there are no longer any substantial restrictions or conditions on my right to receive my interest in the partnership capital.

The Partnership in Operation

Steve: OK. Suppose we get a partnership in operation. Since the partners will pay the income tax on partnership income, is the partnership required to file a federal return?

Mike: Yes, the partnership must file a return—IRS Form 1065—but it is for informational purposes only. A civil penalty is now imposed on any partnership that fails to file a complete partnership information return, unless reasonable cause is shown. The penalty consists of $50 times the number of partners for each month that the failure continues, up to 5 months. This penalty is in addition to criminal penalties for willful failure to file a return, supply information, or pay tax.[12] The form is due 3 1/2 months after the partnership fiscal year ends. Under Code provisions the partnership tax year must be the same as the principal partners' (partners owning 5 percent of more of capital or profit interests), unless a business purpose for a different tax year can be established. Since most individuals are calendar-year taxpayers, most partnerships also will have a calendar-year reporting period and file their informational return on April 15 each year.

Steve: Let's discuss how the partner is taxed.

Frank: Each partner must include in his or her return for each taxable year his or her distributive share of the partnership income or loss items. Each partner's share of partnership income and loss is computed with regard to what was realized in the taxable year of the partnership.

Steve: Could you be more specific as to which items would be includible as distributive shares?

Frank: The partners must include in their individual tax returns their shares of the partnership income or loss. They must also take into account (and report on their 1040s) a number of separate partnership items,[13] including

- capital gains and losses
- Section 1231 gains and losses
- charitable contributions
- dividends received by the partnership from stockholdings

The partners would then add their share of each of the above items to their individual income and deductions. For example, one partner's share of partnership capital gains and losses would be added to his or her personal capital gains and losses. In the same way, a partner's distributive share of the firm's charitable contributions is added to his or her individual contributions, and the charitable contribution deduction limitations are applied to the total.

Steve: How do the partners determine who gets what, that is, how are the distributive shares of each item determined?

Mike: Generally speaking, the distributive shares of each item are to be determined in accordance with the partnership agreement. If the partnership doesn't cover a particular item, the partner's distributive share of that item is the same percentage as his or her percentage share of partnership income or loss.[14] If the partner would normally receive one-third of all profits and losses, he or she would receive one-third of all capital gains.

Sometimes partners, through the partnership agreement, attempt to shift an item to the taxpayer in whose hands the item will be most beneficial. This allocation of one type of item to the partner who can obtain the greatest tax benefit (such as an allocation of all depreciation deductions to the highest tax bracket partner) may be ignored by the IRS. If such a provision does not have "substantial economic effect,"[15] the partners' shares of that item will be readjusted by the IRS just as if the partnership agreement contained no provision as to the item; that is, each partner's distributive share of that item is determined in accordance with his or her share of partnership income or loss.

It's difficult to determine the distinction between an acceptable and unacceptable allocation. Generally the dollar amounts of income received by the partners must be substantially affected by any special allocations independent of tax consequences.

If the economic aftertax consequences to one partner are enhanced by an allocation, the economic aftertax consequences to some other partner or partners should be diminished if the allocation is to be treated as having substantial economic effect. Using present value concepts, this principle is applied for calculating economic consequences over the course of a number of years. Treasury regulations state the application of these principles in detail. Those regulations need to be studied in detail to determine the effects of any special allocations that the partnership may be considering.

If special allocations do not satisfy the requirement of substantial economic effect, they will usually be allocated in accordance with the general provisions in the partnership agreement for sharing income and loss.[16]

With respect to contributed property by the partner to the partnership, the partnership will generally be required, rather than permitted, to allocate *built-in* gain or loss on contributed property to the contributing partner, and not in accordance with each partner's interest in the property.

Steve: Suppose that one partner feels his or her distributive share of partnership income is too little compensation for the efforts provided. Can that partner obtain some type of salary from the partnership?

Frank: Yes, a partner can obtain a salary or, as it is sometimes called, guaranteed payment. A guaranteed payment is a sum paid to a partner, regardless of whether the partnership has income. This payment is deductible by the partnership.

Guaranteed payments are ordinary income to the recipient partner. Perhaps an illustration of the treatment of guaranteed payments would be helpful. Ethan, a partner in the Ethan Ward partnership, is to receive a payment of $10,000 for services, plus 40 percent of the taxable income or loss of the partnership. Assume that after deducting payment of the $10,000 salary to Ethan, the partnership has a loss of $8,000. Of this amount, $3,200 (40 percent of the loss) would be Ethan's distributive share of partnership loss. In addition, Ethan must report as ordinary income the guaranteed payment of $10,000 made to him by the partnership. This guaranteed payment would be reportable by Ethan in the taxable year of the partnership in which it deducted the payment and that ended with or within Ethan's own taxable year.

Steve: Suppose a partner wants to sell his or her partnership interest 2 or 3 years after the partnership is in operation. The amount received on the sale minus his or her basis in the partnership will be taxed. Is that partner's basis in the partnership interest the same as his or her original basis?

Frank: No, the partner's basis will not be the same.

A partner's basis is increased by the following three factors:

1. his or her capital contributions
2. his or her distributive share of partnership income
3. his or her share of liabilities "assumed"

A partner's basis is also reduced by the following three factors:

1. his or her share of losses
2. his or her distributions or draws
3. his or her share of liabilities *relieved*

Steve: Let's see if I understand. When a partnership is formed, the basis of a contributing partner's partnership interest is (1) the amount of money plus (2) the adjusted basis of the property he or she contributes to the partnership.

This same rule applies to a new partner who contributes money or property. The initial basis of a partner who receives an interest as an inheritance is basically determined by valuing the interest at the date of the decedent's death. If an individual acquires a partnership interest by gift, the new partner's basis would be the same as the old donor-partner's basis plus any gift tax paid on the transfer.

If a partner loans money to the partnership, that partner's basis is increased by his or her share of the partnership's liability to him or her as an outsider.

If only services are contributed, and the contributing partner receives an interest in partnership capital (that is, an interest in the property contributed by his or her copartners), then the contributing partner realizes current ordinary income as long as there are no substantial restrictions on that partner's right to withdraw or dispose of his or her interest in partnership capital. When such income is realized, that income will be added to the partner's basis.

Abe and Benny open a delicatessen. Abe owned luncheonette equipment with an adjusted basis of $4,000 and a fair market value of $5,000. He entered into an agreement with Benny in which Abe would contribute his equipment to the partnership and Benny would contribute $5,000 in cash. By mutual agreement, each man will own a 50 percent interest.

Since the adjusted basis of Abe's property was $4,000, the basis for Abe's 50 percent interest is $4,000. On the other hand, Benny's basis is equal to the cash he contributed, which is $5,000.

Of course, the original basis is only a starting point. If we had to determine the basis of a partner's partnership interest one year after the formation of a partnership, we would have to adjust the original basis to reflect changes that have occurred.

We'd start with the original basis—increase that figure by any subsequent capital contributions, and also increase basis by the sum of the partner's share of the partnership's taxable income as well as its tax-exempt receipts. So, for example, if the partnership received life insurance death proceeds, this cash would serve to increase each partner's basis.

Since an increase in a partner's share of liabilities is treated as if cash had been contributed, a partner's basis increases to the extent of his or her share of increased partnership obligations, such as accounts or notes payable and mortgages assumed.

Next, we'd reduce basis (but not below zero) by the amount of a partner's share of partnership losses, distributions by the partnership to the partner, and by the amount that the partner's share of liabilities was decreased.

Suppose the two of you formed a partnership. This year the firm lost $10,000. Frank's distributive share of the loss was $5,000. If the adjusted basis of his partnership interest, before considering his share of the partnership loss, was $2,000, he could claim only $2,000 of the loss this year. The adjusted basis of his interest would be reduced to zero. An individual partner's loss deduction cannot exceed his basis for his partnership interest at the end of the year for which the loss occurred. However, the partner is entitled to an unlimited carryover of nondeductible partnership losses.

If your partnership realized an $8,000 profit next year, Frank's $4,000 share of that profit would increase the adjusted basis of his interest to $4,000 (if we don't take into account the $3,000 excess loss he could not deduct last year). Next year's return should show his distributive share of partnership income to be $1,000 ($4,000 distributive share less the $3,000 loss he was not allowed to take this year). The adjusted basis of his partnership interest at the end of next year would be $1,000.[17]

What's the purpose for those increases and reductions in basis?

Mike: When we increase a partner's basis, what we're doing in effect is shielding those amounts from a subsequent tax. For example, when you sell your partnership interest, you should not have to pay tax on income you've already paid tax on. By the same token, your share of the tax-exempt income (such as life insurance proceeds) received by the partnership should be considered an additional capital investment by you—so if you sell your partnership interest, you should not be taxed on that item, either. Likewise, if you assume a portion of the partnership's liabilities, it's the same as if you contributed a like amount of cash. You should be able to recover that amount of cash tax free.

Reductions in basis serve just the opposite purpose. By reducing basis, you account for recoveries of basis on capital invested in the partnership resulting from losses deducted against other income, distributions of property or money from the partnership to you, and decreases in your share of partnership liabilities.

Partnership basis is important in determining the amount of loss that can be recognized. It also affects taxation upon the disposition of a partnership interest on a partner's retirement or death.

Tax Effects upon Retirement or Death of a Partner

Steve: Let's examine the tax effects when a partner retires or dies.

Mike: I think it's best to do this in two stages. Let's first talk about a sale by the retiring or deceased partner to his or her former partners or to an outsider. Later, we will discuss payments from the partnership itself to the retiring or deceased partner's estate or other successor in interest.

When a partner's interest in a partnership is sold, his or her gain (that is, the amount received minus that partner's basis in the partnership interest) is taxed. Such gain will be treated as all capital gain, unless a partnership has substantially appreciated inventory or unrealized receivables.

Unrealized receivables are essentially uncollected fees and other rights to income. The term includes the right to payment for (1) goods delivered (that were not capital assets or would not be treated as capital assets on a sale), or (2) services, to the extent that these rights are not currently includible in income under the partnership's method of accounting.[18]

Items are considered *substantially appreciated inventory* if their fair market value is equal to more than 120 percent of their adjusted basis to the partnership.[19]

In the event that a partnership has substantially appreciated inventory or unrealized receivables, the selling partner must fragment his or her gain into both a capital-gain portion and an ordinary-income portion. The selling partner's share of the potential gain on substantially appreciated inventory, if sold, plus the partner's share of unrealized receivables, is taxed as ordinary income.[20] As previously mentioned, the balance is capital gain, including payments for goodwill. The remaining partners have the option to increase the basis of partnership assets in proportion to the gain recognized to the retiring partner.

Upon the sale of a deceased partner's partnership interest, the basis to his or her estate or successor in interest will be the value of the partnership interest (other than the value of unrealized receivables) on the date of that partner's death.[21] Any unrealized receivables will be taxed as income in respect of a decedent.[22] The partnership can make a special election under another section of the Code that allows adjustments to the bases of certain items held by the partnership.[23]

Frequently partners will enter into a buy-sell agreement that states that on the death of a partner, the surviving partner or partners will purchase the deceased partner's interest. To fund this cross-purchase-type agreement, often each partner acquires, pays for, and is the beneficiary of a policy on each other partner's life. The premiums each partner pays are not deductible. The insurance proceeds, however, will be income tax exempt.

Steve: Is there some way that the partnership can buy a partnership interest? I'm thinking of something similar to a stock redemption in the corporate area.

Mike: Yes, the partners may agree that the partnership will buy, or as it is sometimes called, "liquidate," a partner's interest. Generally the partners enter into a buy-sell agreement, which states that upon the death or retirement of a partner, the partnership will purchase the former partner's interest. To fund this type of agreement, partnerships purchase life insurance on the lives of their individual partners. Premiums paid by the partnership are not tax deductible, and the insurance proceeds, when received, will be income tax free.

Steve: How is the retiring or deceased partner taxed when payment is received from the partnership for his or her interest?

Mike: If the partnership purchases a retiring partner's interest, the purchase price and the partner's share of the partnership basis in assets must be broken down into several parts. The purchase price and basis of the partnership in its assets must be segregated into amounts attributable to

- partnership property
- substantially appreciated inventory
- unrealized receivables
- goodwill

There are now two different ways in which the payments are taxed. In a partnership in which capital is not a material income-producing factor (a service partnership), the liquidation of a general partner's interest is taxed in four layers.

First, that portion of the purchase price attributable to partnership property, exclusive of substantially appreciated inventory, unrealized receivables, and goodwill, must be determined. If the retiring partner receives an amount for his or her interest in partnership property that exceeds that partner's share of the partnership basis in such assets, he or she will have a capital gain. The remaining partners have the option of increasing the basis of partnership assets in proportion to the gain recognized to the retiring partner.

Second, the retiring partner's share of the potential gain on substantially appreciated inventory will be treated as ordinary income to the recipient. The partnership increases its basis for these inventory items in the amount that ordinary income is recognized.

Third, the portion of the purchase price attributable to unrealized receivables of the partnership, such as accounts receivable that were not previously taxed as partnership income, is taxed as ordinary income to the recipient, but is deductible by the partnership.

Fourth, the portion attributable to goodwill can be treated in one of two ways: If the partnership agreement states that payment will be made for goodwill, the recipients will report any gain as capital gain, but the payment is not deductible by the partnership. Of course, the amount paid for goodwill must be reasonable. If the agreement is silent as to goodwill, the payment is taxable to the recipient as ordinary income and is deductible by the partnership. In the case of such agreements, the Code treats any other amounts paid as "additional payments."[24] Additional payments are treated as ordinary income to the retiring partner. They are characterized as part of the retiring partner's distributive share or as a guaranteed payment to the retiring partner. Of course, amounts that are treated as part of the retiring partner's distributive share or as a guaranteed payment are not taxed to the remaining partners. Another way to look at this is that the partnership obtains a deduction for the amounts paid to the retiring partner. In this type of situation, the retiring partner prefers the partnership agreement to state that payment will be made for goodwill to ensure that capital-gains treatment will be obtained. The remaining partners prefer the partnership agreement to be silent as to goodwill, so the partners can obtain a deduction for the payment of additional payments. This issue must be negotiated by the partners. Often the retiring partner is willing to receive ordinary income rather than capital gain and allow the other partners a deduction, if a greater amount is received for his or her interest. Note that, in general, a partnership has no basis in its goodwill for tax purposes unless it purchased the goodwill in a taxable acquisition. In such cases, the partnership can amortize its cost for the goodwill over a 15-year period, thereby reducing its basis in the goodwill.

In the event of a liquidation of a deceased partner's interest, the partner's basis in his or her partnership interest will be increased to its date-of-death value under the rules for inherited property as discussed previously.

In the case of a liquidation of a partnership interest other than that of a general partner in a service partnership, both unrealized receivables and goodwill are automatically treated as partnership property. As a result, the partnership in such cases receives no deduction for payments for such property. This is a different rule than that which applies to a service partnership. There is also no deduction to the partnership with respect to payments for substantially appreciated inventory, although a basis adjustment is made corresponding to such payments as in the case of a service partnership.

To the extent the partner receives more for his or her interest in the partnership's cash and other property than the partner's share of basis in those assets, he or she will have a capital gain. The remaining partners have the option of increasing the basis in partnership assets for the gain so recognized by the partner. However, any portion of the payments received for unrealized receivables and substantially appreciated inventory that exceeds the partner's share of partnership basis in such assets is treated as ordinary income. The retiring partner must segregate the cash and other property from the substantially appreciated inventory and unrealized receivables.

TABLE 1		
	Adjusted Basis	Fair Market Value
Cash	$ 9,000	$ 9,000
Real estate	30,000	36,000
Accounts receivable	0	30,000
Goodwill	0	45,000
Total	$39,000	$120,000
Liabilities	0	0
Capital accounts		
A = $ 40,000		
B = 40,000		
C = 40,000		
Total $120,000		

Steve: Could you give me an example of how these rules operate?

Frank: Assume that Catherine wishes to retire from the Cartland partnership, a service partnership which utilizes the cash-basis method. Assume that Catherine's basis in her partnership interest is $13,000. Assume that the balance sheet of that firm on the date of retirement may be stated as in table 1 above.

Assume that Catherine is willing to sell her interest for $40,000 cash. If her other partners purchase her interest, her taxable gain is $27,000. Catherine's gain is treated as a capital gain except for amounts attributable to her share of unrealized receivables and substantially appreciated inventory.

This firm has no substantially appreciated inventory. Its only unrealized receivables are its accounts receivable. Catherine's share of the unrealized receivables is $10,000 (1/3 x $30,000), and since the partnership basis in the unrealized receivables is zero, $10,000 of her $27,000 gain must be treated as ordinary income. The balance is capital gain. The remaining partners have the option to increase the basis of partnership assets in proportion to the gain recognized to the retiring partner.

Mike: If the partnership decides to liquidate Catherine's interest for $40,000, Catherine still has a $27,000 gain. However, her amount received must be fragmented into $15,000 for partnership property (1/3 x [$9,000 cash + $36,000 real estate]); $10,000 for unrealized receivables (1/3 x $30,000 of accounts receivable); and $15,000 for goodwill (1/3 x $45,000).

TABLE 2 Taxation of Payments to a Retiring Partner or Deceased Partner's Estate			
Nature of Partnership Asset	Type of Buy-Sell Agreement	Estate of Deceased or Withdrawing Partner	Partnership, Remaining, or Surviving Partner
Capital assets (cash, build- ing, equip- ment, furni- ture, etc.)	Entity and cross purchase	Capital gain/loss	No deduction
Unrealized receivables (service part- nership)	Entity and cross purchase	Ordinary income	Deduction
Unrealized receivables (nonservice partnership)	Entity and cross purchase	Ordinary income	No deduction
Substantially appreciated inventory	Entity and cross purchase	Ordinary income	No deduction
Goodwill	Cross purchase	Capital gain/loss	No deduction
Specified goodwill (ser- vice partner- ship)	Entity	Capital gain/loss	No deduction
Unspecified goodwill (ser- vice partner- ship)	Entity	Ordinary income	Deduction
Goodwill (non- service part- nership)	Entity	Capital gain/loss	No deduction

There is no substantially appreciated inventory. The payments for (1) partnership property, (2) unrealized receivables, and (3) goodwill are taxed as follows:

- *Partnership Property:* Catherine receives $15,000 for her share. Her basis in her partnership interest that is allocable to those assets is $13,000. She has a $2,000 capital gain. The remaining partners have the option to increase the basis of partnership assets in proportion to the gain recognized to the retiring partner.
- *Unrealized Receivables:* Catherine receives $10,000 for her share. Since the partnership has no basis in this asset (cash-basis taxpayers have a zero basis in accounts receivable), neither does Catherine. The $10,000 would be ordinary income to Catherine and the partnership would have a $10,000 deduction.
- *Goodwill:* She receives $15,000 for her share. Since the partnership has no basis in this asset, neither does Catherine. If the partnership agreement states that payment shall be made for goodwill, then Catherine may treat the $15,000 as capital gain. If the partnership is silent as to goodwill, Catherine will treat the $15,000 as ordinary income. If Catherine does have ordinary income, then the partnership may treat the $15,000 as part of Catherine's distributive share or a guaranteed payment to her.

If instead Cartland is not a service partnership, the cash and other property consists of one-third of $9,000 cash, $36,000 real estate, and $45,000 goodwill, or $30,000. Catherine has one-third of $30,000 unrealized receivables, or $10,000. As she has no basis in the unrealized receivables, she recognizes $10,000 ordinary income. The partnership has no deduction. Catherine recognizes a $17,000 capital gain on the excess of the $30,000 attributable to cash or other property over her $13,000 basis.

A summary of the foregoing is shown in table 2.

Taxation of Limited Partnerships and Their Partners

Steve: Can we discuss the taxation of a limited partnership?

Frank: Basically limited partnerships and their partners are taxed the same as general partnerships and their partners. As you know, a *limited partnership* is an arrangement in which the liability of some of the partners is limited to what they have contributed to the partnership. This is a useful device when a number of individuals are investing in an enterprise, but only one or a few individuals will be the managing and active members. Generally the limited partners are limited in authority as well as liability.

The major question presented in most problems relating to limited partnerships is whether the *partnership* is in reality an association taxable as a corporation. Once a determination is made that a given organization is a limited partnership, the taxation of the business and its partners follows the same general rules we have already discussed.[25]

Taxation of Family Partnerships and Their Partners

Steve: Can you explain how the taxation of *family partnerships* differs from the taxation of other types of partnership?

Frank: A family partnership is one whose members are closely related through blood or marriage. The family, for this purpose, includes only husband or wife, ancestors, and lineal descendants, and any trusts for the primary benefit of such persons. Brothers and sisters are not included.

Family partnerships are not essentially different from other partnerships. However, because family partnerships are sometimes formed solely to shift income within a family unit in order to minimize taxes, such partnerships receive special scrutiny both as to initial formation and actual operation.[26]

If there is economic (non-tax-motivated) reality to the arrangement, the partnership allocations of income will be accepted for income tax purposes. If the arrangement lacks economic reality, the Internal Revenue Service may ignore the entire partnership arrangement and reallocate income to properly reflect the interests of the partners.

There are certain guidelines designed to test the reality of the partnership arrangement. For example, in the determination of whether income can be shifted from the original sole proprietor to a new partner, a family member will be recognized as a partner only if his or her capital interest was acquired in a bona fide transaction (even if by gift or purchase from another family member), where capital is a material income-producing factor. To be treated as a partner for tax purposes, the family member must actually own the partnership interest and be vested with dominion and control over it.

Capital is considered a material income-producing factor if a substantial portion of the gross income of the business results from the use of capital (as when substantial inventories or investments in plant, machinery, or equipment are required).

If a family member acquires a capital interest in a family partnership by gift in which capital is a material income-producing factor, there are limitations on the amount that may be allocated as his or her distributive share of partnership income.

First, the donor of the interest must be allowed an amount that represents reasonable compensation for services rendered to the partnership. The remaining income generally may be divided among the partners according to their agreement for sharing partnership profits and losses. However, that portion of the remaining income allocated to the donee may not be proportionately greater than that allocated to the donor on the basis of their respective capital interests.

An interest purchased by one member of the family from another member of the family is considered to be created by gift for this purpose. Let me give you an example. A partnership in which the father sold (considered a gift) a 50 percent interest to his son had a profit of $60,000 for the year. Capital was a material income-producing factor. The father performed services worth $24,000 as reasonable compensation, and the son performed no services. The $24,000 must be allocated to the father as compensation. Of the remaining $36,000 income attributable to capital, at least 50 percent, or $18,000, must be allocated to the father since he owns a 50 percent capital interest, and the son's share of partnership income cannot exceed $18,000.

Steve: What happens when capital is not a material income-producing factor?

Mike: An individual can still be treated as a partner for tax purposes even if capital is not a material income-producing factor. However, in such cases the individual must contribute substantial or vital services.

Capital is not a material income-producing factor if the income of the business consists principally of fees, commissions, or other compensation for personal services performed by members or employees of the partnership. A law or accounting practice would be a good illustration. For a son to be recognized as a partner in his father's accounting firm for tax purposes, he'd have to contribute substantial services to the business. Otherwise, his share of partnership income would be reallocated by the IRS to the other partners.

Steve: In this brief review of the income tax treatment of partnerships, it's apparent to me that the area is quite complex, and that each situation merits thorough as well as thoughtful consideration and planning.

Mike: That's correct, but with proper structuring, the partnership is often the best means of conducting a profit-motivated undertaking when more than one individual has an interest. The benefits, however, may not be available if the partnership exists merely on a handshake, with no analysis, planning, or formalization of the understanding of the parties. For income tax purposes, a partnership may exist in such a situation, but it is likely that problems will arise in the future, without carefully thought-out and formalized arrangements.

NOTES

1. Internal Revenue Code of 1986, Sec. 7701(a)(2).
2. Treas. Reg. Sec. 301.7701-2(a).
3. Uniform Partnership Act Sec. 31.
4. Uniform Partnership Act Sec. 9.
5. Uniform Partnership Act Sec. 15.
6. S corporations are an exception to this rule.
7. An attempt to prevent a "disguised sale" by the partner to the partnership was the objective of the amendment of IRC Sec. 707(a) by the Tax Reform Act of 1984. If a

transaction is characterized as a sale, then the partner would be acting as a nonpartner for this one transaction and, of course, would be required to recognize a gain or loss on the transaction.

8. IRC Sec. 721.
9. IRC Sec. 722.
10. IRC Sec. 752(b).
11. Treas. Reg. Sec. 1.721-1(b)(1). (A capital interest in a partnership means an interest in its assets that is distributable to the owner of the capital interest upon the owner's withdrawal from or the liquidation of the partnership. The mere right to share in the earnings and profits is not a capital interest in the partnership.)
12. IRC Sec. 6698(a) and (b).
13. IRC Sec. 702(a).
14. IRC Sec. 704(b).
15. IRC Sec. 704(b)(2).
16. Treas. Reg. 1.704-1(b).
17. Where a partner cannot practicably determine the adjusted basis in the partnership interest, the adjusted basis of his or her interest may be determined by reference to the partner's proportionate share of the adjusted basis of partnership property, as long as it is reasonable that the result produced will not vary substantially from the above basis rules. IRC Sec. 705(b); Treas. Reg. Sec. 1.705-1(b).
18. IRC Sec. 751(c).
19. IRC Sec. 751(d).
20. IRC Sec. 736.
21. IRC Sec. 1014.
22. IRC Sec. 691.
23. IRC Sec. 754.
24. IRC Sec. 736(b)(2).
25. See Treas. Reg. 1.752-1(e) for an important exception to this statement concerning liabilities incurred in leasing or real estate partnerships.
26. IRC Sec. 704(e).